Dirty Feet

How the great unwashed created the Tour de France

Les Woodland

McGann Publishing
McMinnville, Oregon

Published by McGann Publishing
P.O. Box 864
McMinnville, OR 97128
USA

www.mcgannpublishing.com

ISBN 978-1-7367494-0-1

Table of Contents

1
Départ fictif

The départ fictif *is the point at which riders first turn the pedals, but without actually racing. It's a relaxed parade to get them safely through a city centre and to make sure that everyone is together, that any laggards have caught up, and that the show can begin. One year, a Dutchman called Rini Wagtmans broke that rule and attacked right from the start. Mayhem broke out. His plan was to get out of sight in the winding roads of the city and then hide up a side street. Then, he thought, he'd tag along at the back and enjoy the spectacle of 200 rivals chasing nobody at all. The problem was that the rivals flew by so fast that he found himself left behind and had to spend a long time riding hard to catch the chase that he himself had initiated.*

It's not what you'd call normal behaviour. Nor do you expect to read it in your daily paper. And yet it happened: each morning after a race meeting on the new Parc des Princes bike track in parkland to the west of Paris, you could find a newsletter column headed *Pieds sales.* It means "dirty feet" and it listed all the competitors who'd gone home the previous night without a shower.

That says a lot about Henri Desgrange. He's the man who took the credit for thinking up the Tour de France and he's certainly the man who invented a sport: multiple-day cycle racing on the road, or stage racing as it became known (a stage being originally the overnight stop, as in the old expression "to make a stage somewhere"). Even into old age, he was obsessed—there is no other word—with physical exercise. Those who worked with him on early Tours knew better than to be seen doing nothing on rest days: Desgrange would insist not only on running up and down scree-covered mountains, but also that any unfortunate official he saw ought to join him. Even as he was dying slowly and painfully, he insisted on rising from his bed and timing how long it took to shuffle from one side of his room to the other.

Desgrange set himself a formal rule in life, to submit himself to his daily physical exercises. He had to commit himself, according to his draconian theories, to a violent effort, prolonged, repeated, going sometimes as far as pain, needing tenacity and even a certain stoicism. He was on a crusade against Original Inertia, against the numbing effect on the body of a civilisation that more and more made effort unnecessary. He made himself an apostle in a battle to maintain character. Suffer and sweat! That meant a culture of permanent individual effort, of cross-country running at least three times a week in the park at St-Cloud.[1]

Desgrange was convinced that France would be a better country if everybody did as he did. Which included having a shower.

2
Départ réel

The départ réel *is the end of the rolling start, the point at which the lions enter the arena and the gladiators are expected to fight for their lives and the amusement of those looking on. In bygone days, nothing much happened. The starter dropped the flag and the riders ambled on until it suited someone to have a go. And then, depending on the status of whoever broke the peace, the rest of the field would wave them goodbye for a few hours or they would chase straight away. That changed when television began covering all the day's racing instead of the last hour or two. The big stars were no more inclined to get puffed out than they had been before, but the presence of cameras was a chance for lesser lights to clear off up the road and justify their contracts by exposing the embroidery on their sponsors' jersey until, inevitably, they were caught soon before the end.*

Nobody remembers Alfred Cornié now. It may be that nobody much knew him at the time but, back then in 1893, he announced that the end of the nineteenth century was "the age of the bicycle."[2] It was an extraordinary thing to be able to say because only thirty years earlier, in 1863, the Michaux family had built only two *vélocipèdes*. And the Michaux come into the story because, in an alleyway—no longer there—off the avenue Montaigne in Paris, they first put pedals to wheels and thereby invented the bicycle.

At the start, what we now call bicycles were hobby-horses, heavy wooden structures sometimes even with a carved horse's head, that the rider straddled and walked along with his feet—animated walking, if you like. Not only could they not be pedalled, they couldn't easily be steered. That, though, didn't stop Karl Drais, the man credited with its invention, from walking his *Laufsmaschine* the fourteen kilometres from Mannheim to Szchwetzingen.[3] It took him only a little more than an hour and no man had previously travelled so fast under his own efforts.

Now and then you see the Michaux family's road written as the avenue Montagne, as though there were mountains between the Eiffel Tower and the Paris ring road. But in the French style of honouring the notable by naming a street after them, the avenue Montaigne celebrates a philosopher, Michel de Montaigne. And philosophy is taken seriously in France to this day, so that no student taking his *baccalauréat* will succeed if he hasn't started by passing his *philo*.

The avenue Montaigne runs now as it ran then, from the Eiffel Tower to the pont d'Alma, where Diana, Princess of Wales, died in a car crash in the underpass in August, 1997. Nowadays, the avenue is the swanky address of expensive shops, fashion houses and many of the finance companies whose names are intentionally too little known to those who pass that no more than a small polished plate announces their presence. Then, though, it was a noisy street of traders, hawkers and small workshops of the sort in which Pierre Michaux worked.

Michaux first lived in Bar-le-Duc, which is halfway between Paris and the German border further east. He was born there in June, 1813, and his father, Louis—who couldn't read and who accepted the spelling Michaut when it was presented to him[4]—signed the birth certificate with an X.[5] Pierre became an office boy in the ironwork business when he was fourteen. He showed talent and eventually became a master blacksmith. There was only so much money in that, though; if he wanted more, he'd have to become a coach-builder. And to do that, he set off on his Tour de France.

Cyclists visiting France sometimes get excited when they see a street name referring to this Tour. They take a picture of it, marvel that the race could pass along so narrow a road, and then if they go further and check race records, their puzzlement is complete when they find the race never did visit the town. To their disappointment, this Tour de France was a tradition that existed before the race began and which continues now. It's the circuit that apprentices make, to work for a succession of masters and learn their trade as they go: one forge in one town, then a little later moving elsewhere to a new master.

Dirty Feet

Pierre travelled round the south and then the west, thought himself competent and quickly bought a carriage works when he got back to Bar-le-Duc. His prospects delighted a girl called Marie Louise Perrine Cauret, six years younger than he. They married, had a daughter, Maria, and then in August, 1842, a son whom they named Ernest Henri Charles. The children prospered but not the carriage business, which folded up. Pierre needed a job to keep Marie, Maria and Ernest, let alone himself, fed and clothed, and he found it with a carriage-maker in Paris. He stayed there for a year and a half and then set up by himself just off the avenue Montaigne, beside number 29. It's not worth going to find it. Number 29 is now the obviously expensive Paris headquarters of the Harry Winston jewellery business. But it was there that Alfred Cornié's "age of the bicycle" was born.

To be exact, Michaux made the metal bits of carriages—the chassis and the springs—and not the cart, if it was industrial, or the compartment and upholstery if it was for the rich. He banged metal for a living and took on whatever jobs he could find. It's easy now to underestimate the scale of the business that he was in. Horses pulled, horses carried and, as it happens, horses piled up dung and spread urine wherever they went. Which was everywhere. It became such a problem that it was debated, without a solution, at international conferences. And with reason, because London had 50,000 horses on the street every day. New York had 100,000. Paris had fewer but it was also a smaller city, so the density was the same.

Legend says that a writer on *The Times* of London predicted that "in fifty years, every street in London will be buried under nine feet of manure." *The Times* even quoted itself in 2017 without naming the source, which I'd wanted to find.[6] In the end, frustrated, I wrote to *The Times*. Surely the paper wouldn't misquote itself, I said. Harry Wilson, the banking correspondent who wrote the reference that I read, rightly took it as a light-hearted inquiry and now, also intrigued, bothered the newspaper's archivists with it. It was probably a welcome break from their everyday work and they turned up a leader column on the subject and even a letter from Randolph Churchill, the father of Winston, but no forecast of manure higher than a man.

"There is a very simple answer to your question," Harry wrote back. "You have not been able to find a reference, because no such article exists… It appears that the reference I picked up, and many others, is apocryphal and is presumably a product of some long ago misunderstanding/wrongful attribution. It has been fascinating to go back through the archives and examine this." *The Times* printed a *mea culpa*, saying my suggestion that it surely wouldn't have misquoted itself turned out to be precisely what it *had* done.

VOICES FROM THE PAST

My invention consists in the arrangement of two wheels, the one directly in front of the other, combined with a mechanism for driving the wheels, and an arrangement for guiding, which arrangement also enables the rider to balance himself upon the two wheels. By this construction of a *vélocipède*, after a little practice, the rider is enabled to drive the same at an incredible velocity with the greatest ease… What I claim as new and useful, and desire to secure by Letters Patent, is: The combination and arrangement of the two wheels A and B, provided with the treadles F and guiding-arms D, so as to operate substantially as and for the purpose herein set out.

—Letters patent no. 59 915, dated 20 November 1866. Michaux's mechanic, sometimes credited with fitting the first pedals, was Pierre Lallement, born at Pont à Mousson near Nancy in 1843. While he was staying in the USA, he and a James Carroll of New Haven, Connecticut, patented a pedalled bicycle there in November 1866. But by then the Michaux were not only selling their machines in Paris but were close to selling their company to the Olivier brothers. The row continues among cycling historians.

Anyway, the point is that there were an unbelievable number of horses and the things they had to pull and that therefore there was a lot of work for a competent mechanic in the heart of Paris. And it's here that things get going because—and this is a bit vague as history and it's changed a lot in the telling—we are at the happy start of the bicycle and also of a sad story.

In true friend-of-a-friend manner, a journalist called Louis Baudry de Saunier said that someone called Boit told him that he had gone to

Michaux and his son in 1855—ten years before de Saunier was born—along with his *draisienne*, the bicycle that had be scooted with the legs. According to de Saunier, "the coach-builder's son, having tried out the *draisienne* two or three times in the rue [*sic*] Montaigne, near the Cité Godot de Mauroy where his father was then living, suddenly wondered whether, without putting feet to the ground, it would be possible for a man to trundle himself along without falling, as a hoop did when it was bowled...

"The crank, although so simple, had not entered the head of any experimenter during the past forty years and would without doubt still have been lacking after 1855. Why had it appeared? Inspiration cannot be commanded. It came to Ernest Michaux like sunstroke, without warning."[7]

There are several versions of this story and historians still fret over them. One, told by Michaux's other son, Henri (or sometimes Henry), says it was a hat-maker called Brunel who brought in the *draisienne*. But the upshot is that Michaux's accidental invention made the family fortune. Napoléon III bought one and the Prince Impérial, Louis-Napoléon, gave a dozen to his friends. There are pictures of him riding in the park at Compiègne north of Paris with his cousin, the son of the Duke of Albé.

Michaux turned out more and more bikes and, not the first amateur businessman to overreach himself, needed money because he could now go neither forward nor back. He turned to two brothers: the straight-haired René and the curly-haired Aimé Olivier, the nephews of a rich chemicals magnate from Lyon, who lent him 50,000 francs. And in time and because Michaux didn't repay his debts, the Oliviers' vaguely named Compagnie Parisienne in the avenue Bugeaud took possession of the Michaux works.

The avenue Bugeaud runs south-east from the Bois de Boulogne and the Oliviers' building, at number 12, still stands, a five-storey place with a metal-fenced balcony on the middle floor and a large, double wooden door for access from the street. A plaque beside the door says that, presumably among other occupants, the building is the offices of lawyers. On the other side of the road is a glass-fronted centre for dental and hearing problems. In 1869, riders gathered in the street there before setting off for the new Arc de Triomphe and the uncertain start of Paris–Rouen, the world's first town-to-town cycle race.

Michaux lost his business but then opened up in opposition. That was foolish enough but he made the still greater error of using the very name he had just lost to the brothers. The Oliviers sued for 100,000 francs, twice what they had originally loaned. The end came when the Germans shelled Paris in a siege as part of the Franco-Prussian war in 1870–71. The factory was destroyed as 12,000 shells fell in twenty-three nights. Michaux was ruined. He died in a pauper's hospital at Bicêtre on the southern edge of Paris in 1883. Ernest died the year before him, aged forty. There is a memorial to them both at the junction of the rue Maginot and the rue du Bourg at Bar-le-Duc.

And this is how we get to Henri Desgrange. We reach him because he was convinced that France had lost the Franco-Prussian war because of the country's sickly youth. It was not a fear unique to France. It also happened in Britain, where generals insisted the country would have fought better in the Boer War in South Africa had the army not had to reject so many recruits because of their malnutrition and underdevelopment.[8] The English physique, a report showed, was markedly weaker than fifty-five years earlier: 105 men in a thousand had been under 5 feet 6 inches in 1845, but by 1900 that had risen to 565 per thousand. The army finally had to take men as small as 5 feet.[9] Recruiting sergeants could tell a candidate's social origin from the state of his limbs and teeth. Some parts of Britain were so deprived that nine out of ten applicants were rejected.[10]

The French were in a similar position. Half of all children died before they were ten. Life expectancy, taking that into account, was just twenty-five. Few reached what we would now consider middle age. Smallpox was a great killer. Vaccines raised life expectancy to thirty by 1800, then thirty-seven in 1810, but it fell again to less than thirty by 1865 when Desgrange was born.[11]

It's difficult now to imagine how hard things were. The thousands who worked in the clothing industry were so little because of malnutrition that they couldn't themselves buy clothes small enough. The archives brim with complaints of even better-off workers wearing the soles of their shoes until they vanished and then having to walk the streets shoeless.[12] Their houses were poorly ventilated and damp and had no running water. Migrant workers sometimes slept twelve to a room on hard planks. Established workers could have a room on the top floor of a building but probably sharing with another family.[13] In the countryside, Martin Nadaud near Limoges lived with his family and their livestock, humans and animals sharing the same front door. Only a partition separated them inside the house, the animals on one side and the family cooking and sleeping in the single room on the other. Animal feed often dropped through the rafters from the loft above their heads.[14]

The historian Iva Polansky says that "in the old houses, water had to be carried up from the courtyard and in the newer buildings the taps ended on the fourth floor because there was not sufficient pressure in the pipes. There was no heating; a portable stove on which a stew would be cooked was rarely used as fuel was too expensive."[15]

Desgrange's mission was to create a France in which it could never happen again. He would create—although it wasn't his idea— a race that would turn out a superman to inspire the callow, shallow-chested youngsters he saw around him. His race would set off physical and moral regeneration, "waking up hundreds of kilometres of countryside asleep with physical inaction", to stimulate "emulation, energy, willpower."[16] In an odd way, and not at all as he intended, his wish eventually became true. But that is a long way ahead in our story.

When it's said, as it is so often is, that Desgrange's ideal Tour de France would be one in which only one man had the strength to finish, that was exactly the case. As Geoffrey Wheatcroft says: "These first Tour men were far from physical wrecks but they have the unmistakable proletarian appearance of their time, gnarled and knotty."[17] The man who survived better than the rest would be a superman, more than three decades before an American comic book gave him his face.

Henri Antoine Desgrange, whose twin Georges-Léon looked like the duller sort of librarian—which indeed he was, because he worked with unresented dullness in a newspaper archive—was born at 5 a.m. on the last day of January, 1865, in the boulevard de Magenta, at number 118. The street is named after a battle in Italy six years before Desgrange and his brother were born. Their father was a builder and architect called Jacques and their mother was Marie-Hortense.

They lived a street away from the Gare du Nord, Europe's busiest station, from which Eurostar trains now leave for London. The modern street has four lanes in each direction, the outer pair reserved for cyclists, buses and taxis. It's lined by banks and a pizza restaurant, with apartments and offices on the upper five storeys, the buildings all stone in the style of the Haussmann remaking of Paris. Number 118 is sandwiched by a Domino's Pizza branch and a business offering help with visas, residency permits and translations.

Nobody then could have realised that Henri would grow up to claim credit for the Tour de France. Not then and not for a decade and a half later because he wasn't a cyclist from the start. He came to cycling, as many have done, because he wasn't good enough at anything else. His first affection, while he was studying at the College Rollin,[18] was for swimming, an affection not at all matched by his talent. He "battled in an altogether anarchic fashion to coordinate the beating of his legs with the alternate projection of his arms; he looked, alas, like a man drowning" observed an amused colleague who watched him.

Then he turned to running, the love of which never left him. At fifty-five he won the Cross des Ancêtres cross-country. And in 1891 he saw his first bike race, the finish of the monster ride from Bordeaux to Paris, the first time it had been held. What he made of it we'll never know. There seems no record of his emotions and certainly not what he thought of the race's being won by an Englishman: George Mills. British riders, indeed, took the next two places as well, having insisted before the start that they would compete only against fellow amateurs. This is a point worth making because throughout his life Desgrange was an enthusiast for professionalism in sport, in contrast to Pierre de Coubertin, the founder of the modern Olympics, who wanted nothing but amateurism. The two were born only two years apart.

Around 1890, Desgrange joined the Amicale Vélo Amateur in Paris and eventually became its treasurer. He is still in the records as a holder of the world hour record. A lot is made of that but the truth is less exciting: the International Cycling Association, the forerunner of the Union Cycliste Internationale, had only just standardised its records. Whoever rode first at each distance inevitably became the first record holder. However slowly Desgrange rode, his name would be first provided nobody tried before him.

He rode 35.3 kilometres on 11 May 1893, using the Buffalo track in Paris—named after the cowboy showman, Buffalo Bill, who'd put on a spectacle there. The track will return to Desgrange's story a little later. He rode in a sleeveless dark jersey with a dragon printed on its front, in shorts that came to his knees, and with shoes like a child's buckled slippers. His hair was dark and his face lean with a generous moustache that spread, like the lower limbs of a Christmas tree, wider than his chin.

Long after the record, and not long before his death, Desgrange remembered: "Under a blue sky, I mounted a bicycle weighing a good twenty-five kilograms with tyres an outrageous 500 millimetre diameter, a gear of 4.70 metres[19]... As a measure of prudence, I slung a bottle of milk from my handlebars, in case of bonk.[20] When I got off the machine at the end of sixty minutes, I wasn't only the world record man for the hour on a bicycle, I was an object of horror to the people who took care of me after my 35.325 kilometres. I was filthy, streaked with oil and snot, covered with dust; in short, nobody would touch me with a pair of tongs. My director bought me lunch at the Porte Maillot, a sumptuous meal, 2.50 francs a head; he also offered me several bank notes which I could cash for gold louis. Because of my amateur status I refused instantly. But my God! How happy I was."[21]

History goes better and credits him permanently with the world 100-kilometre tricycle record, a record not much contested at the time and never again since. The reference to refusing gold coins, because he was an amateur, casts doubt on the more frequent reports that he had become a professional.

His hour distance lasted until 31 January the following year, his birthday, when Jules Dubois of Pontoise rode 38.2 kilometres. He was by far the better rider, having established world records at 100, 200, 300, 400 and 500 kilometres in 1892, although under the old, unratified system. His successful attempt on the twenty-four-hour track record in July, 1892, ended after a little less than twenty hours but did bring him records at distances from 100 to 500 kilometres. He died after a cycling crash in 1928, long after his career was over. He was sixty-six, having been a runner, a cyclist, a car racer and finally a pilot.

Desgrange worked in the offices of the Depeaux-Dumesnil law company in the rue des Batignolles near the Place de Clichy. He is often described as a legal clerk but the truth is that he qualified and practised at the court of appeal, confirmed by legal documents held by his family.[22] Legend goes further and says that in 1882 he was fired for cycling to work with bare calves. A client, a woman, had seen him in the street and felt shocked.[23] The story is much told but without any evidence. More likely is that Desgrange wasn't much good at his job, whatever it was, and it was even more likely that his abrasive personality grated on the partners in charge. An offended woman may have been involved but the story is probably of bosses despairing of a young man keener on bicycles than the law. If Desgrange told the story himself, it was better than "They fired me because I was arrogant and useless."

Type *Desgrange + mollets nus* into a search engine—*mollets nus* is the French for "bare calves"—and it brings back nothing. Try the same at the national library, the Bibliothèque Nationale de France, and the outcome is no better. So could it be a story better known to English-speaking fans than to the French themselves?

He did keep some of his legal nous, though. When he gave autographs once he became famous, he always signed at the top of the page, "so that nobody can write above it and make it look like a contract."[24]

Desgrange and the Michaux family were contemporaries. Both lived through the Franco-Prussian war. Desgrange was just a boy. He probably understood little of the political causes but, as he grew older, he could not have escaped the outpouring of explanations of why France lost. Desgrange knew all that, and the thought was still with him when he left the law company and picked his way through life by writing cycling articles "of a virulent causticity"[25] and fairly soon by running a bike track.

The background to that is that a balding, round-faced and moustachioed aristocrat called Herbert Osbaldeston Duncan was one of several young Englishmen with time and money to spare, who came to Paris to try their hand—or their legs—at cycle racing. It was the fastest sport on earth, faster even than horses, and it would stay that way until motor racing arrived around 1900.

Duncan, who was known to friends as H.O.D., was a classic British amateur, the sort of man who—like the country's Olympic officials—believed that only those with a private income could be true amateurs for only they would be untempted by money as prizes. His grandfather had been a cricketer, steeplechase champion and master of foxhounds for the Quorn hunt in Leicestershire. The old boy died penniless thanks to his love of colourful living, but his own son had all the money he needed; income tax in Britain had been tried, then abandoned. Herbert, the grandson, lacked neither money from the day he was born, in London, on 22 November 1862, nor the talent for spending it. He lived in a more than respectable house in Notting Hill, then just beyond the western edge of London, while his father lived in some style at West Drayton, now a suburb somewhat degraded by the low-flying jets making their way in and out of Heathrow airport.

Herbert became interested in cycling when he was at Taplow College, on the Thames west of London, and in 1878 he joined the Belgrave cycling club when he was sixteen. And there he fell in with bad company. He was cycling in London when he met two French riders, Frédéric de Civry and Paul Médinger, who were profiting from the impression that another Frenchman, Charles Terront, had been making on the track there. De Civry spoke good English and Duncan became so much of a friend that they rode together and de Civry blew "a plated bugle... much to the discomfort of other neighbours."[26] Duncan travelled between Britain and France several times before living first in Montpelier and then in Paris.

At eighteen, he became a professional. You can imagine the horror that caused in the family home. And not just horror, because the family spoke of treachery. The boy was unrepentant and he travelled to Italy to race with de Civry and Médinger and then returned to Britain to win what was billed as a fifty-mile grand prix on a track at Leicester in April 1886.

By then Duncan was a businessman as well as a competitor and he had several bike shops. On brochures, he was described as a director of the Rudge bicycle company, at 16 rue Halévy in Paris, a building that is now a branch of the Caisse d'Epargne bank. He joined Rudge in 1867, travelling to France in the hope of orders.[27]

His dream was to build a track in Paris. There was no chance of asking his family for the money and so he had to look elsewhere. De Civry suggested he try Clovis Clerc, the director of the Folies Bergère cabaret. Clovis saw the possibilities because he had a showman's flair and he had been impressed by Buffalo Bill's Wild West Show. With Duncan, he chose to put the track at Neuilly-sur-Seine where Buffalo Bill had been and, cashing in on the name, called it the Buffalo. What both men needed now was someone to design it. They had heard of a young man called Henri Desgrange, whose freelance writing suggested he knew what he was talking about in an era when few people did, and they gave him the job. Desgrange's design was for a track in concrete with bankings. It was "a track worthy of the name", one report said, even though it had trees near the finish straight.

By then, Duncan had started to look elsewhere. He was seduced by the newly arriving motor cars, noisy and unreliable though they were, and he became a pioneer of car racing. He founded *Motor Review*, became commercial manager of the British Motor Syndicate, which tried to establish a stranglehold on the British car industry by buying the patents to all the spare parts it could, and then moved back to France to run the De Dion-Bouton car company—where he would have an unexpected part in the creation of the Tour de France.[28]

In his absence, the Buffalo became the track of dreams. It was run by a flamboyant playwright called Tristan Bernard, who happened to be the first man in any sport to have the idea of ringing a bell to indicate the last lap. When you see a painting of a man in plus-fours, his beard sticking up at an angle as he stands by the trackside, that is Tristan Bernard. The painter, Toulouse-Lautrec, was one of his most enthusiastic spectators.

Desgrange's design, the track on which he broke the hour records, was broken up to house an aircraft factory in the First World War. But by 1897, he had moved to join a businessman called Victor Goddet in the management of a newer track, the Parc des Princes. For half a century it was the finish of the Tour de France. It is here that Herbert Duncan comes back into our story. We left him, you'll remember, when he abandoned cycling and moved to the De Dion-Bouton car company in 1898, eventually becoming its chairman.

De Dion-Bouton was founded in 1885 by Jules-Albert de Dion of Nantes—who styled himself a count even though aristocratic titles had been scrapped in the revolution of 1789—and the engineers Georges Bouton and his brother-in-law, Charles Trépardoux. Their first idea was to make steam-powered cars, because that was the world that Bouton and Trépardoux knew best. But then they saw their mistake and also the possibilities of internal combustion and that's the way they went. Except for Trépardoux, who couldn't believe that steam wasn't the future, and left. The remaining pair made cars for themselves and for any other company that wanted to put on its badge and boast of them as its own.

It was natural that a company so influential would need to advertise. It bought so much space in *Le Vélo* that it is sometimes described as its largest shareholder. *Le Vélo* started in 1892, a daily paper in the rue Meyer, off the boulevard Haussmann, that reported sport but added general news that it frequently coloured with observations of its own. That much wasn't unusual in those days.

The problem was that France was going through internal divisions that came close to civil war. Behind them was a soldier called Alfred Dreyfus, an army captain from Mulhouse near the Swiss border, and the highest ranking Jew in the largely Catholic army. He had been convicted in 1894 of selling secrets to the Germans from his job at the war ministry. France was still blushing at the Franco-Prussian war, a defeat the army was unprepared to believe was its fault. It followed from that that someone must have passed information to the enemy. Dreyfus was stripped of his rank and sent to the penal colony of Devil's Island off French Guiana.

The evidence was pretty scrappy. The most damning was a piece of paper, which turned out to be forged, and the fact that he came from close to the German border.[29] The right, rural people, the army and the Church (then the power behind the throne) believed he was guilty; liberals, city people and others were convinced that he wasn't. Those on Dreyfus' side included the writer Émile Zola, whose page-long accusation of bias and corruption finally pardoned if not cleared Dreyfus. Among those who hesitated was the president, Émile Loubet, a severe Victorian gent with a full beard and wide moustache. His background was as a lawyer and he wasn't sure the evidence against Dreyfus stood.

Dreyfus was sentenced on 4 June 1899 and next day Loubet had a day out at a steeplechase at the horse-racing course at Auteil. There, too, a little before 3 p.m., was de Dion, a heavily built skirt-chaser, a man of violent temper and with a habit of challenging others to a duel.[30] No one was more convinced that Dreyfus had been rightly sentenced. He foamed in a rage when he saw Loubet, and a man in his group with a blond moustache, Fernand de Christiani, brought his stick down on Loubet's top hat, crushing it and "forcing it over his face like a candle extinguisher."[31] For that he got four years in jail, though some sources say ten.

Le Figaro lamented: "It is hard to think why young people of high breeding and high society [*appartenant aux grands cercles*] should spit on and even attack with a cane a sixty-year-old man who had been invited by the race organisers and who was encircled by the ambassadors of all nations."[32] It was pushing it to call them young people because de Christiani was thirty-five, but the point was otherwise made. De Dion, seeing the way things were going and objecting to a rush of gendarmes insistent on stopping it, joined in by smacking one of them with his cane and losing its bejewelled end. He landed a fine of 1,000 francs and fifteen days in jail.

There he was visited by *Le Vélo*'s editor, Pierre Giffard, a round-faced man with thin dark hair, who was born at Fontaine-le-Dun, near Dieppe, on 1 July 1853, the son of a solicitor. He had come into cycling because of his sick dog. A vet recommended he give it more exercise, that Giffard should ride a horse while the dog ran beside him. Giffard neither owned nor liked horses, so he settled on a bicycle.[33]

He had a spell in the army and then a career at *Le Figaro*. He and de Dion had generally got on together, at least so far as he was prepared to say publicly, because they shared a vision of a world which would fill with cars.[34] Now, though, de Dion was cross because Giffard had criticised him and his other major supporters and because he believed *Le Vélo* was selling advertising more cheaply to his rival, Alexander Darracq—which wasn't improbable because Darracq had helped get *Le Vélo* started in the first place.

At times, *Le Vélo* had published more about Dreyfus than it had about sport. The two argued furiously as de Dion sat in his cell in La Santé jail. Until then, they had each held their silence and fumed. As Giffard had put it, nobody knew more about cars than de Dion but, if they were to remain friends, they were better not discussing politics. This time, though, things went too far. De Dion set out to wreck Giffard, starting with Giffard's efforts to get into politics and by ruining his paper. He'd do that by starting his own sports paper and make a point of not including any general news, let alone comment. It would rub Giffard's nose in the dirt and Giffard would be ruined.

3
Rubbing noses in the dirt

There is a suspicion that de Dion had planned his attack on Giffard well before his stay at La Santé. For all that he claimed well after the event that they had all but broken out the wine and cheese in his cell and agreed like gentlemen to disagree, it seems he had earlier spent 1,000 francs to buy a satirical magazine called *L'Auto-Vélo,* so he could use the name. It was pleasingly close to Giffard's title and sure to confuse buyers. It didn't work; it lost rather than made money.

But who was going to run this new, proper sports paper? The men behind it sold cars and tyres. They could damage *Le Vélo* by pulling their advertising but what did they know about publishing, about anything other than the world in which they worked? Most of those who did know such things were already working with Giffard.

There were, though, two men sulking in the shadows. Desgrange and Goddet wanted nothing more than that their Parc des Princes track should succeed. At thirty-five, in those days already in middle age, Desgrange didn't know where else to turn: the track was his life and his future. He had tried editing a publication called *Paris-Vélo,* which had probably annoyed Giffard, and now Giffard was barely reporting the Parc's races. The track was twice as long as anywhere else, too far from Paris, and not worth his consideration, Giffard sniffed.

And so it was to Desgrange that de Dion made his first tentative suggestion. Would he consider opening a daily sports paper? If he would, de Dion and friends would bring in the advertisers and put up the money.

Desgrange at a distance seems a strong, dictatorial man. And it's true that he was, when he ran the Tour de France. His power was absolute and he enrolled and excluded riders as he chose. His influence ran across cycling generally, so that the Tour de France had what amounted to a permanent chair at meetings of the new Union Cycliste Internationale. Even if he wasn't there, it was important to know his opinions—because he was the sport's most influential figure, an overlord.

But that was later. In 1900, the year the UCI was born, he was far less sure of himself. He had drifted through too many jobs to throw in the one he loved: management of the Parc des Princes. So he said that whatever he did, he would agree only on condition that Victor Goddet came too. Goddet, a quiet man more interested in accounting than sport, was the track's major shareholder and therefore the boss. Desgrange didn't want to break their relationship or to upset him.

De Dion called them to a meeting at his office in the avenue de la Grande-Armée. It was one of the most prestigious addresses in Paris, on the main road that runs north-west from the Arc de Triomphe to the corner of the Bois de Boulogne. All the new car companies were there, slowly replacing the bike shops which had previously reigned. De Dion's home wasn't to be sniffed at either; he lived at 4 avenue d'Iéna in what is now the Iranian embassy.

Desgrange and Goddet really didn't know. If the paper succeeded, they would have all the publicity they wanted for their track. If it failed, which was much more likely, Giffard would show no mercy and, as Desgrange put it, "our poor Parc des Princes will be the loser in the battle." The two spent perhaps an hour with de Dion, then sat together on a bench outside. Goddet's son, Jacques, remembered that their conversation was simple: "What are we going to do? Accept? Refuse?" We know now that they accepted, but it was no immediate decision.

The new paper was called *L'Auto-Vélo*, for two reasons. The first was that it reflected the two crazes of the era: cycling and driving. This was no surprise: the British magazine, *Cycling*, retitled itself *Cycling and Moting*[35] for a while, and only a court ruling prevented the Cyclists' Touring Club from accepting motorists. Much later, the National Cyclists' Union, also in Britain, briefly proposed accepting riders of light motorcycles, and *Cycling* again changed its name, to *Cycling and Mopeds*. The second reason was that de Dion had bought that satirical magazine of that name not with the intention of reviving it—it had published only intermittently—but to annoy Giffard. But it did mean that he owned the title and putting it on the top of a sports paper would surely create public confusion with *Le Vélo* and harm its sales.[36]

Giffard thought so, too, and quickly sued. A judge ruled that de Dion's purpose could only be to create mischief. The paper had barely started and it had to drop the word *vélo* from its name. Some backers may have hoped its columns would carry the sort of news that *Le Vélo* had gone in for, although more to their political taste. But Desgrange stuck to the original plan. In the first issue, he aimed a dart at his rival: "There will never be, in *L'Auto-Vélo*, anything political; oh readers, whatever your opinions, whether you are for or against, you can count on us never to talk to you about it." And since there was no one else, and the backers could put Giffard out of business anyway, they sulked but they agreed.

They were an odd bunch, those backers. One was a Dutchman born in Paris, Thierry Zuylen de Nyvelt van de Haar, an aristocrat who helped form the Automobile Club de France but who never deigned himself to drive a car. Instead, he insisted on being carried everywhere in a horse-drawn carriage. The premises of the club were closed after the Auteil disturbance because the police believed they were the headquarters of a subversive plot. De Dion was for a while followed wherever he went.

Another was Gustave Clément, who made bicycles but then turned to cars and then to airships and for whom Desgrange had briefly worked. He was "more of a royalist than the king", according to the author Jacques Lablaine.[37] And then there was Alexander Darracq, happy to back both sides at the same time. And David Salomons, a member of parliament in Britain and the Lord Mayor of London in 1855, whose father founded the National Westminster bank. When the son became a Sheriff of London (a largely ceremonial position for which he was expected to pay the Crown £300 a year, then a considerable sum), he was refused because the Christian phrasing of the oath offended him as a Jew. That caused a commotion and in the end he was allowed to take the oath but leave out the bits he didn't like.

Better still, there was the self-styled Viscount of Montureux, who nervously told the others that he had none of their achievements but that, if they would give him the time, he would convince them he was worthy to join them. Intrigued, they agreed. And they watched as Montureux unfolded a roll of sketches and calculations and spread them on the table. Solemnly, as the others politely stifled their smiles and gasps, he announced that he was about to go into business manufacturing cars on legs.

The new paper appeared for the first time on 16 October 1900, printed on yellow paper to contrast with the green of *Le Vélo,* and boasting 542 correspondents around France and abroad: a lot more than *Le Vélo.* It cost five centimes an issue, or eighteen francs in Paris for a year's subscription, twenty francs elsewhere. It began with a single-column headline, *Notre Programme*, and a long article by Georges Prade (listed later as the automobile correspondent). It began: "*L'Auto-Vélo* is a product of its times and it is necessary that it appears. We live better and we live faster than before. Generations before ours have known the incivility of college life, the never-ending circuits of the heart of the *lycée* [higher school], the studies without end uninterrupted by healthy fresh air; then, liberated from school, the hardness of daily work…" and on and on before in another long paragraph it said that modern students had life better, that they had sports clubs, football, running… "and there they are outside school, refusing the protection of their mothers' skirt, ready to make their way in life, wherever that may be, be it a long way away, be it in the colonies."

People had more time to read then. Or at any rate Prade thought they had because he went on for four closely-written broadsheet columns so comprehensive that they named not just the editor but the switchboard operator (Paris 227-68), although not the financial correspondent, who was given as XXX.

The first three pages reported sport; the last was advertising. Prominent among those who bought or perhaps negotiated space were de Dion (maker of "small cars, petrol-engined tricycles and quadricycles") and Gustave Clément, who announced in a wordy style that surprises today that Monsieur Rasson, his salesman in Spain, "has just accomplished, given the nature of the roads, a true *tour de force* in driving from Paris to Madrid in his little Clément car."

The writing style was alternately purple and relaxed. One cycling story begins: "I have just heard a curious story of which the hero was the rider, Gascoyne…" It's all rather vague with the passing of time but Gascoyne was cycling with secret papers when he saw an army patrol ahead of him. "He immediately thought of hiding his message. Sliding it into the handlebars of his bicycle was the work of a moment.

The patrol was on him in a second. After conscientiously searching him, but in vain, they took him prisoner. Gascoyne lived for several days with the patrol that had arrested him. And then one morning he escaped with his machine and next day he delivered the message that had been entrusted to him."

The story ended with a celebratory: "Another benefit of the bicycle!"

A correspondent in London reported with mild astonishment that "the freewheel, which is little used in France, by contrast has many fans in England…" Just above it is a report that the Danish champion, Thorvald Ellegaard (whom it names as Th. Ellegaard), was protesting against a suspension of six months and a hefty fine for an incident connected to the Grand Prix de l'Exposition in France. Ellegaard hadn't yet won the first of his six world sprint championships and it looked as though the Union Vélocipédique de France wasn't keen that he should.

Desgrange, strengthened by the caustic articles he had written in *Bicyclette*, began using his editorials to lay into the unsanitary ways of athletes in general and cyclists in particular. He told the French that they were weedy and regretted that France might not have lost the Franco-Prussian war, that Paris would not have been besieged and that the Germans would not have taken Alsace had the country looked after its youth better. As it was, they were in such a poor condition—you'll remember the conditions in which people lived—that the army would have been stronger and more numerous had it not had to refuse so many candidates because of their ill health.

Victor's son, Jacques Goddet, recalled: "He wanted *L'Auto* to be the premier journal of French society… There was no crime in its pages, no obscenity, but a vigorous campaign against syphilis, a taboo subject, against the ravages of this silent shame which, by being hidden, was spreading still further. There were editorials in favour of hygiene, of cleanliness."[38] A cyclist with ambitions, Desgrange wrote in his training manual *La Tête et Les Jambes (Head and Legs)*, should exercise more, lay off sex and have "no more use for a woman than for the previous day's socks."

The first edition of the paper gave its address as 10 rue du Faubourg-Montmartre ("*adresse télégraphique Vélauto-Paris*"), between the Gare St Lazaire and the Gare de l'Est. And there it stayed until, now separated from the Tour de France, it moved out to the suburbs at Issy-les-Moulineaux. It's not the Montmartre that tourists know, by the way, with its windmill, bars and artists; this is the lower Montmartre, an area of "a thousand occupations, of industry, of business and of pleasure."[39]

The street hasn't changed a lot over the years, even if the occupations have. When *L'Auto* took two floors, the other occupants of number 10 were a woman who supplied feathers for hats, several private apartments and "a photographer who stopped only at going to a convent to obtain his models."[40] The floors were connected by a single staircase.

Pictures from the time show horse-drawn carriages, horses pulling trailers, men in suits and hats, a gendarme in cape and kepi standing in the road with his back to the traffic and a street of dirty buildings advertising their purpose. The street was cosmopolitan and it still is, and other than a supermarket that has appeared recently, the rest is probably at least representative of back then: a bar, a small theatre with a canopy, small shops, private homes and upper-storey offices. The archway that led to an earth courtyard is filled now by the electrically sliding doors of the supermarket and that courtyard is filled now with the sort of things you'd buy at any Monoprix in Paris. Other than that, it looks just the same. The high narrow windows are still there on the upper floors, each protected by low railings.

L'Auto was at the back of the courtyard. The walls had the newspaper title in its antique lettering on a large sign above the door and then again below every window sill. On the top floor, immune from the smells of the restaurant at ground level, sat the new editor, a short-tempered man respected by his staff but not always loved. Behind his back they called him Bostock after a forgotten but probably complicated chain of reasoning that linked him to a Victorian lion-tamer who had recently appeared in Paris.[41] Or perhaps it was because Frank Bostock was the first to introduce boxing kangaroos to his performances. In any case, Bostock ran a circus and that may have been enough. The nickname came from a somewhat irritating man called Georges Abran, who had the wearying habit of repeatedly addressing people by imaginary names. It's improbable that he ever dared address Desgrange to his face as Bostock, although it seems Desgrange was aware of it, but just using the name round the office could have been enough.

Dirty Feet

VOICES FROM THE PAST

> [Name] won [a car race] in a Renault with Michelin tyres with the agreement of the first floor.
>
> —*L'Auto* wasn't reluctant to drop in the names of companies that advertised in the paper. The favoured ones were chosen by Victor Goddet, who looked after commercial affairs, and reporters were required to show his approval by writing on the edge of their scripts. But things sometimes reached the printer and then the paper before anyone noticed.

France may have been intrigued by this new newspaper but it was far from enthusiastic about buying it. Not only did *Le Vélo* have the market but there were plenty of other contenders. There was no radio, no television and no paper was likely to accept advertising for a rival. Only word of mouth could increase sales.

The traditional way to publicise a paper was to run a bike race. Other competitions as well, of course, but the advantage of a bike race was that there were many potential winners—just two in a football match, remember—and that they came from all over the country. A soccer match depended on a calendar; you knew one week who was going to play whom the following weekend, or the following month. Bike races brought stars almost haphazardly and they brought outsiders and regional hopefuls known in their home town if not always anywhere else. Every race was an original and each rider's form and hopes could be debated for weeks, even if they hadn't yet entered.

More than that, bike races covered unbelievable distances in an era when most people had been little further than their own village or town. People wanted to see super-heroes who could ride such distances and, in the first races, they could spot the favourites and the gallant no-hopers because they passed for the most part one by one. And then again, you could only know what happened before and after a race passed your house by buying the next day's paper. So you were hooked.

Most of the big races we still have today were started more as commercial ventures than a desire for human competition. And they were part of a noble tradition. As the American historian Bill McGann observes: "In the nineteenth century newspapers used a multitude of devices to increase their sales. Much of what both Charles Dickens and Alexandre Dumas wrote was serialized in newspapers. People breathlessly bought the next day's edition to learn how the Three Musketeers or Oliver Twist would get out of the fix the authors left them in at the end of the last installment."

And not just fiction: "In the USA, Darwin and Hattie McIlrath, sponsored by the *Chicago Inter Ocean* newspaper, went on a three-year trip around the world by bicycle while the paper printed weekly reports of their progress. Newspapers would often create their own news, for which they were the only suppliers in an era before radio and television."[42]

Literature wasn't going to work for Desgrange and he had forsaken finding juicy news scandals, true or invented. All he had was bike races. And his imagination failed him. He was good at taking other people's ideas and not objecting to being credited with them but he had less talent for coming up with his own. So when one paper ran a race, all he could think of was to run a bigger version of the same thing—which, if only by comparison, gave the rival paper as much and maybe more publicity than his own.

Sales had begun to rise but then they stuck. Desgrange needed many more than the 20,000 papers he sold each morning. Only at 25,000 would the paper start to break even. *Le Vélo*, at four times the daily sales, looked invincible. It was also a fair bet that many who bought *Le Vélo* bought *L'Auto* as well, as an extra. Advertisers are quick to spot things like that and, having spotted them, to conclude that there was no point advertising to the same reader twice in the same day and that they may as well stick to the paper that sold better. The fact that *L'Auto* had heart-raising peaks after it promoted races but that sales quickly returned to what they had been before suggests again that *L'Auto* was an afterthought, an extra rather than a first choice.

The second edition had been predictably enthusiastic about the success of the first. "Even before the first *L'Auto-Vélo* came off the presses to bring *la bonne nouvelle sportive*, I received exactly 1,257 letters from people anxious and curious what editorial line our newspaper was going to follow", said a signed leading article. They were different times, of course, but even if we wonder that 1,257 people would be so tense with excitement that they'd buy a stamp to write to a paper they hadn't yet even seen, the tone is of a great wave of subscriptions ready to fall on 10 rue du Faubourg-Montmartre. There may have been a good dose of talking up the story.

The colder truth is that *L'Auto* couldn't make a profit and that the investors weren't happy. And we know they put pressure on the paper generally and its editor in particular because several sources confirm that there was a crisis meeting on the second floor on the morning of 20 November 1902. Two years after the paper began, it should have been doing better. Desgrange, investors were saying, may not have been their best pick.

This meeting has been much romanticised. The classic version is that Desgrange said "What we need is something to nail Giffard's beak shut" and that a silence had followed in which all those around the table remembered the failure of what they had tried before. Accounts of the meeting agree on the theme but not the details. And that's hardly surprising because *L'Auto* was not likely to report its own crisis meeting. If minutes were kept, they vanished when all *L'Auto*'s paperwork and all that of the Tour de France were moved south to escape the German invasion of 1940, never to be seen again.

What is agreed is that Géo Lefèvre, a twenty-six-year-old rugby writer whom Desgrange had poached from *Le Vélo,* tentatively said something like: "Let's organise a race that lasts several days, longer than anything else. Like the six-days on the track but on the road."

Lefèvre, a bespectacled, square-faced man, was probably the youngest there. And as a rugby writer and not a businessman, he was out of his depth. He says it was Desgrange who replied but others say it was Georges Prade, the man who had written the first leading article, the one that took the trouble to name the paper's switchboard operator. One or the other hesitated and then said: "If I understand you right, *petit Géo*, you're proposing a Tour de France."

"*Et pourquoi pas?*", Lefèvre is supposed to have answered—"And why not?"—an answer that suggests as much nervousness as it does confidence.

The idea meant something to Desgrange. He had been impressed when, in 1895, Théodore Joyeux, a barber born in Castillonès, a hilltop village in the south-west of France, had ridden 5,500 kilometres to tour France in nineteen days, averaging 289 kilometres a day. In an era of primitive bikes and mainly unsurfaced roads—not to mention often unclean drinking water—that was quite a feat. Especially since his bike had no brakes, no gears, not even a freewheel because the wheels were turned by a rack and pinion connecting the pedals to the back wheel. The significance of riding round France was clear to Desgrange and he said as much to the regional daily paper, *Sud Ouest*, in 1921.[43]

If there were other suggestions, they've vanished with time. Much of cycle-racing is its romance, especially in this epic era when as much was invented as was genuine. Attendance at all sports was good, and much higher than in the television age, but cycling was advancing steadily. Desgrange and the others couldn't see the future, of course, but they had it on their side. France introduced a bicycle tax in 1893 and for the first time there were figures more dependable than those of bike factories, which had their own reason to exaggerate.[44]

Since 1891, Pierre Giffard's Paris–Brest–Paris had enthusiastically adopted the quest for a superman by demanding its participants pedal 1,200 kilometres largely without sleep. But a Tour de France, in its sporting sense, was something new. As we've seen, many a visiting modern-day cyclist stumbling on a road name or another reference to the Tour de France has been disappointed to find it referred not to the race but the far older tradition of apprentices learning their trade in a succession of cities. One of the most popular books in France, *Le Tour de la France par Deux Enfants*, had delighted the country since 1877 with the adventures of young André and Julien. More than six million had been sold. But, with a good dose of romance, it was probably that morning in the early winter of 1902 that the words "Tour de France" were first spoken to describe a bike race.

Desgrange was intrigued but doubtful. But he had no other ideas so this wasn't the moment to turn one down out of hand. This being France, a country in which Lunch Happens, he invited Lefèvre to join him. As Jacques Goddet assessed with a wry smile in his memoirs: "It was rare gesture which eloquently demonstrated the shock [of the Tour idea] suffered by a man extremely rigorous about expenses."

The two left the building, ignored the restaurant on their own ground floor, turned left and walked up a slight rise, then turned right into the boulevard Montmartre and entered a restaurant a little further on the right. There's some debate whether it was called the Café Madrid or the

Taverne Zimmer but in any case it later became a branch of TGI Fridays. The staff there are so convinced that that was where Desgrange and Lefèvre ordered lunch that at the back of the bar to the right they created a small display: an old black bicycle, although markedly not one that was ever ridden in a race (it has mudguards and an open frame of the sort used by women and long-frocked parsons), a couple of black-and-white photos and a few enamel advertisements. It's on a panelled wall above small square tables, with a plaque to celebrate "*la plus grande compétition sportive du monde*", although nobody knows now just where the two men sat.

Ever since, historians have pieced together—and largely invented—the conversation that followed. One says that the two talked little, that Lefèvre was nervous and had no idea whether his idea was going to make his career or sink it. It had been the first thing that had come into his head, he said long afterwards, feeling that he ought to contribute at least something. Only when the espresso arrived is Desgrange supposed to have said: "Explain this idea of yours." So Lefèvre went through it, thinking aloud, adding ideas as they came to him. It would be a race so colossal that nobody could outdo it. It would follow the edges of France and finish in Paris. It would pass through so many towns and villages that sales would be guaranteed throughout the country.

"And the cost?", Desgrange is supposed to have asked.

"The towns will welcome the publicity", Lefèvre suggested. "They may pay the costs for us."

Desgrange apparently hesitated again. His heart was in track racing and he'd long been sniffy about races on the road. In any case, he was powerless without Goddet's agreement and Goddet was even more parsimonious than he was.

"He needs to be convinced," Desgrange said. Now, where once Lefèvre had been worried, it was Desgrange. Flagging sales already made his paper and his position on it insecure. An idea that horrified the investors, still worse cost them intolerable sums, would end his career. The two went to see him. Goddet listened without interrupting, according to his son, "and, without hesitating, to their deep surprise, handed them the keys to the safe, which never left him, and said simply: 'Take whatever you need.'"

There are two ways to read this story. One, the better known, is that Goddet was won over. The other is that "Take whatever you need", and the theatrical gesture of handing over the keys, was cynical. Goddet was tight-fisted in life and business[45] and the paper was broke. There was little to take—the point that he was making according to this other interpretation—and even if there had been he wasn't the sort to enthuse at hare-brained ideas. It was, after all, only after an anguished discussion on a public bench that he'd taken the job in the first place and it was as an investor and a bookkeeper that he had taken a share of the Parc des Princes.

Those who say that Goddet was saying that the budget was unlimited for an idea he had only just discovered are perhaps missing the point. Enthusiastic he may have been but only because, if there was no money, there was no money to lose. Or, alternately, that if there was a small amount of money, it may as well be spent on a Tour de France because nothing else had worked. The atmosphere may well have been pessimistic, not enthusiastic.

We'll never know.

4
Big news

Three days after *L'Auto-Vélo*'s name was legally and reluctantly truncated to *L'Auto*, the paper announced this new Tour de France. It would be "the biggest cycle race ever, Toulouse–Bordeaux–Nantes–Paris—20,000 francs in prizes—starting 1 July, finishing 5 July at the Parc des Princes." Most papers enthused at best, reported it at worst. *Le Vélo* gave it a scant mention without naming the rival that was organising it. Giffard had won the battle of the paper's name and pocketed the damages that a court had awarded him, but the wound was still open.

In the years surrounding this first Tour de France, Queen Victoria died, Marconi sent his first transatlantic radio message, Australia was established, Henry Ford was opening his first factories, William Harley and Arthur Davidson were wondering if there was a living in motorcycles, and the Wright brothers flew the first aeroplane after working out the theory in their bike shop in Dayton, Ohio. Oscar Wilde died and was buried in Paris, four years after the Klondike gold rush. Above all, Paris held the Olympic Games and the World Exhibition and the Eiffel Tower was built.

The Tour de France may have been small amid all this innovation but it couldn't have chosen a more inventive and productive time. And according to one historian and philosopher, Desgrange was simply developing the French notion of a circuit, a tour of France that dated from the days of Catherine de' Medici who went round France in 1559 after the death of her husband, Henri II, to introduce her two sons to the French and legitimise them for the succession. "This circuit ingrained itself in the national consciousness," he wrote with a pomposity with which Desgrange would have felt comfortable, "and Desgrange understood that perfectly. With the Tour, he created places, set up monuments, created landmarks and promoted the bicycle as a sophisticated product of French industry, an image he carried into the remotest corners of the country."[46]

Desgrange fancied himself as another Zola, France's greatest literary figure and the man whose newspaper accusations spiced up the war over Dreyfus. Desgrange never hesitated to draw in historical characters, no association being too overblown to add glory to his race. Describing the crowd that watched the Tour finish on 15 July 1903, he wrote that it "clapped its hands as the riders passed, in the way that the crowd once saluted, on their return from Spain or Austria, Napoleon's troops."

Of Lucien Petit-Breton in 1908, he said: "He not only knows what he has to do but he will do it! And as Bonaparte—and let nobody ridicule me for comparing the two—said at the Tuilerie gardens as he showed a map of the Po valley and the Marengo plain, 'This is where I will beat Monsieur de Mélas', Petit-Breton duly showed before the stage how he would defeat his adversaries."

Paris, he wrote one day, would be the "enormous octopus whose formidable tentacles attract all to her, whose power, despotic, allows no compromise." But being a Parisian, he said, did not blind him to the special day from Marseille to Bordeaux, where—and he listed the towns—the people did not yet know just how great was the race that was about to descend on them.

Don't underestimate the significance of that. France was a highly centralised state. Paris dominated everything. Until the 1970s the south-western regional manager of a national bank would work not as he would now, in Bordeaux, but in Paris. And there his desk would be next to that of his colleague, the manager for the north-east. Paris still dominates the country but much regionalisation, local autonomy and investment has taken place since. In the days of the first Tour de France, Paris sucked in money and talent and refused to send it back. Provincial cities were sad, abandoned places drained of talent. And the countryside, for France was strongly a rural economy, was left to go to ruin. We have already seen the living conditions of those who lived there.

"At the start of the nineteenth century," say the philosophers Jean-Luc Boeuf and Yves Léonard, "French people had a poor understanding of the geography of their country. Maps were rare and little used, even at school. The physical image of France and its contours remained unknown to the majority of French people."[47] As an illustration of that, the book about the two children making their personal Tour de France—a book, you'd think, that begged for an illustration of the route—didn't have a map until its 1905 edition. By then five million people had bought it and even more read it without having or at any rate getting any idea of just where they went, of what their country looked like.

You can imagine, therefore, the surprise and curiosity that *L'Auto* created when from 1903 it began printing maps of France, the idea of France being a hexagon—now a common expression but not current until the 1960s—being emphasised by the Tour's keeping as close as it could to its boundaries. Boeuf and Léonard go further: they say maps of the Tour unknowingly prepared the French for the end of their empire. They reason is that *L'Auto*'s maps showed only the mainland; even Corsica wasn't shown, let alone the colonies and what are now the dominions and territories, such as Guadeloupe and Tahiti. Until then, like the British, the French had seen themselves at the heart of an empire that reached across most of the world. Even now, after former colonies opted to stay part of France, the country has more time zones than any state on earth.

Desgrange's maps may just have been drawn that way for nothing more than editorial simplicity. But, say Boeuf and Léonard, they soon popularised "a virtually hexagonal image of France, a France amputated since 1903 of not just its *provinces perdues* but also of its overseas possessions and of Corsica, which the Tour did not visit for a century and didn't even figure on maps of the race. When, with the decolonisation of the fifties and sixties, the national space contracted to the point of being for the most part just the hexagon to which few people referred at the time, the Tour had prepared the country—and prepared it for decades—for the retraction of French space to its European and continental—hexagonal—boundaries."[48]

The historian Jim McGurn agrees, saying that Desgrange "later claimed that it encouraged a sense of national identity, establishing *La Patrie* in clear geographic terms."[49]

At the very least, if *L'Auto*'s maps were the only ones that most Frenchmen had seen, they could only have confirmed the identity, continuation, the entity of France after the loss of Alsace-Lorraine and the offence of being invaded and the capital reduced to eating a circus elephant during the Franco-Prussian war. Not that that there was a map when the paper announced the race on 19 January 1903. The news, with the small, simple headline "Le Tour de France," filled the first column with small, dense type and then seven lines of the next. In those days journalists designed their pages from the top left corner and the news ran down one column and then back up into the next until it had taken the space that it needed. No design, no photos, just two sketches of cyclists.

L'Auto's commitment to its new race came just before the riders left the Réveil Matin at 22 rue Jean Jaurès, Montgeron. The bar, now a restaurant, still exists. A plaque on an outside wall announces

ICI
devant le Réveil Matin
le 1er JUILLET 1903
fut donné le départ du
1er TOUR DE FRANCE
organisé par HENRI DESGRANGE

L'Auto ran its headline the width of the front page—"*Le Tour de France Le Départ*" and then, in smaller letters, "*Organisé par L'Auto du 1e au 19e Juillet 1903*"—above a hand-drawn map of France and the Tour's route spread over the middle three of five columns. The race had expanded to nineteen days because riders refused to take part unless they had rest.

"Road racing on the scale of the Tour de France was not an arena sport to be enjoyed for its skills and its shapely, obvious drama," wrote Geoffrey Nicholson. "It was a series of tales brought back from the mountains and related by the riders themselves, the newsmen and just a handful of impartial witnesses. The tales were of disaster and deprivation, treachery and honest courage, extremes of heat and cold, and the triumph over man and nature. These were Giants of the Road, and their exploits required the truth of legends not of newsreels. The Tour de France had to have epic quality."[50]

If epic quality was called for, Desgrange could supply it. And he did. It's hard to know whether his words read as dramatically comical then as they do now but there's no denying he put his back into it. Writing of Paris–Brest–Paris on 5 April 1901, he dipped his pen in purple ink and let rip. And as you read it, remember that the race hadn't actually started…

"There are four of them. Their legs, like giant levers, will power onwards for sixty hours; their muscles will grind up the kilometres; their broad chests will heave with the efforts of the struggle; their hands will clench on to their handlebars; with their eyes they will observe each other ferociously; their backs will bend forward in unison for barbaric breakaways; their stomachs will fight against hunger, their brains against sleep. And at night a peasant waiting for them by a deserted road will see four demons passing by, and the noise of their desperate panting will freeze his heart and fill it with terror."

It produces a smirk now but France loved it then. "The Tour developed a heroic canon that was reflected in the dramatic stories of its riders. The French lionised heroes who embodied cherished masculine qualities that seemed threatened in modern times… The French cherished defeat as much as triumph, as long as there was nobility," says Eric Reed, associate professor of history at Western Kentucky University.[51]

When Desgrange announced that the Tour would start and finish in Paris, it was the first the *préfet de police*, Louis Lépine, had heard of it. He wasn't impressed. Not only did Desgrange's post bring barely any entries—the cycling world had ruled it too far and the rewards too small—but now Lépine was saying that cycling was a disruptive, hooligan sport that would never be held in Paris while he was in charge. Desgrange argued, putting every reason he could, but Lépine was firm. *Non.*

Nobody knows why Desgrange hit on starting the Tour instead at Montgeron, except that he couldn't start it within the boundaries of Paris and that he may have been to Montgeron on bike rides. A guide to the area said it wasn't a bad place to go but it would be better without all the cyclists. The village is now a suburb of Paris, although with a distinct air to it. It stands twenty kilometres south-east of central Paris and less than four kilometres from Orly, Paris's second airport.

The village has existed since at least 1147, the year that it's mentioned on a parchment at St-Maur abbey as Mont Gisonis. The Réveil

Matin bar there stands on the junction of the roads to Corbeil and Melun. In 1796, the two drivers of the Lyon mail coach were murdered in the village for the 80,000 *livres* (currency, not books) they were carrying, much of it belonging to the army. As if that weren't enough, an innocent man was subsequently guillotined—Joseph Lesurques, a blond man just 1 metre 60 tall and unfortunately matching the description of one of the thieves. That was all that was needed.

He and two others were sentenced to beheaded on 3 October 1796, despite the protests of the thieves themselves that Lesurques was innocent. Only then did the law start to have doubts. The true blond man was found and discovered to have, yes, a strong resemblance to Lesurques. But unlike Lesurques, he confessed. Go to the Père Lachaise cemetery on the edge of Paris and you can find his tomb in division eight, with the inscription "He was victim of one of the most awful human errors" His case is frequently cited by campaigners against the death sentence. More recently, people still talk of the day in 2010 that a villager cut his wife's throat "from one ear to the other" in their kitchen.[52]

Faced with the same Parisian ban at the end of his race, Desgrange drew a line across the road outside 147 rue de Versailles in Ville d'Abray, about as close to the Paris limits as he could get. It's about halfway between the river Seine that marked the edge of administrative Paris and the glories of the old royal palace at Versailles. The town is a favourite for *internautes* (the clever name for internet fans) who scour Google Earth to spot a Dassault Mirage fighter jet in a car park. It's there to celebrate the suburb's association with the aircraft industry, the speciality of a college since closed.

The Père Vélo restaurant stood at number 147 and the owner renamed it the Père Auto for the occasion. Once it must have been quite the place. François Mitterand used to favour a table near the fire in the days before he was president.[53] Now it's an Italian restaurant, Il Boccaccio. It looks like a private house set back from the road with double gates at the entrance, low at the hinges and chest height where they meet in the middle. The house is pale cream with a blue and white canopy over the door. The old Père Vélo has long gone. In 1903 it stood on the street itself, two storeys, wider than it was high. There's a commemorative plaque at Il Boccaccio.

Dirty Feet

Photos of the last day of the Tour show a long blue, white and red banner the width of the building, fastened every metre or so such that it hangs in gentle swoops. The national flag hangs from the windows and from those of the Salon de Sociétés next door. A banner on the building announces that it is the *contrôle d'arrivée*. Another, across the road, announces the same thing in old-fashioned typefaces and with *L'Auto* printed as ever in extended Gothic lettering.

Crowds stand to face the bar, uniquely men and all in hats, often white boaters with colourful bands. Several are in baggy plus-fours scooped in beneath the knee, which suggests they have come on bicycles. Several bicycles are visible in the photos. It's hard to decide if the racers have yet to arrive or if they're inside, washing and getting ready for the ceremonial ride to the Parc des Princes which was all the police chief would tolerate.

It was called a *contrôle*, a check, because that's how the race was run. Riders could be two hours apart on the road. There weren't the staff or even the volunteers to stand and wait and turn them the right way. Desgrange had rumbled that and said that "we plan to exercise an extraordinarily rigorous surveillance, especially at night, to enforce the rule banning pacemakers and *soigneurs*. We have already adopted three forms of surveillance—which we are keeping secret—which we know will guarantee the best results. And more than that, we've received a great many offers from friends in the areas the race crosses to keep a secret eye on the race." But it was eyewash. Instead, riders were given a list of towns they were expected to pass, and addresses at which they were to sign a check sheet, but apart from that they were on their own, on trust. They just had to follow the road signs, made easier by the way the Tour kept to the single main highway. Maybe there'd be someone to watch, more probably not.

Club cyclists couldn't keep up and there weren't enough cars in all France to manage constant surveillance. Renault made its first car only in 1898 and, while there were 30,000 cars in France by 1900—almost half the entire world's production—that was for a population of 40 million. Or, put another way, one car, lorry or whatever for each 1,333 people.

There was no small stress in finding a control. Imagine the exhaustion of the distance. Try to imagine a stage, like the first of 1903, that covered 476 kilometres in eighteen hours for the fastest, more for the less fleet. Imagine the distress of being in a strange city, surrounded by excitable crowds speaking in what then would have been heavy and perhaps unintelligible accents. Maurice Garin, that year's winner, said that "The 2,500 kilometres that I've just ridden seem a long line, grey and monotonous, where nothing stood out from anything else. I suffered on the road, I was hungry, I was thirsty, I was sleepy, I suffered, I cried between Lyon and Marseille. I see myself, from the start of the Tour de France, like a bull pierced by the *banderillas*, who pulls the *banderillas* with him, never able to rid himself of them."

Well he might have suffered. Bikes from that era are still around but it's hard to get to ride one. That was something I had the chance to do thanks to a lean, bespectacled man called Alistair Skinner who from his home in the English hunting county of Leicestershire was hoping to sell what he believed though couldn't prove was a bike ridden in that first Tour de France. He had bought it from an elderly Frenchman who had no more use for it.

"It's the forks that catch you out," he warned me. "The rake is enormous, so the first thing that happens when you sit on it is that the wheel will turn sideways and the bike will swing round backwards. It's so long [the whole bike] that I hang it on the rack that supports my other bikes and it touches the floor, whereas the others are well short."[54] It measured 190 centimetres from end to end, 1 metre 18 between the axles. The frame tubes were heavy and set in uncompromising lugs. The chain stays were a single wide tube as they left the bottom bracket and then they divided in a curve to accommodate the back wheel. I wished I'd thought to ask what it weighed.

The bike had no brake. You stopped by pushing back on the pedals in the hope of locking the inch-pitch chain, the links twice the length of a modern chain. The wheel hubs fit into simple slots, the rear pair opening backwards so the wheel could be slid to tighten the chain. The head badge, though it was newer than the frame, said "Cycles Chavigny, Blois." Chavigny is a common name in Blois, in the Loire valley, and there are still companies of that name there, although no bike factory. In any case, Skinner suspected it was a Peugeot.

"I'd love to know who rode it," he said, "but it's impossible to know." Somebody tall, at any rate, because it's a 24-inch frame.

Officials did their best to see the riders didn't cooperate with each other, as competitors would today, and above all that they weren't paced. Until then, many races had pacers, usually on tandems but even on motorbikes or in cars, to "bring out" the competitors. Races behind huge motorbikes were the thrill of track meetings and spectators wanted speed, not subtlety.

Competitors arriving alone at a control sometimes hid the pen to delay others, or spilled the ink. If they'd do that where there were sure to be judges, you can only guess what went on out on the road. And, sure enough, by the following year they were tying wires to cars and being towed by corks held between the teeth, invisible to judges at night and looking for all the world as though there was nothing but effort to account for the grimace and the unusual speed. One or two extended the concept of cycle racing to include catching a train, something for which three were caught as they came out of Dijon station only to find a race official standing by chance at the exit. This stress told on Garin and doubtless others. Late in life, he used to wander the streets of Lens, his adopted home near the Belgian border, demanding in his unhappiness "*Où est le contrôle? Où est le contrôle?*" Where is the control? Where is the control?

Often he would wander into the town's police station, from which he'd be led gently home to the rue de Lille.[55] Garin and a roomful of others were disqualified from the second Tour, which Garin had won, for bending the rules just a little too far.

A neighbour, then a boy, remembered: "He was in no way an adulated hero and even less a rich champion; he spent his retirement running the Antar service station in Lens, where he sold petrol, bicycles and sewing machines. I don't remember any special celebration in his honour, no television teams arriving from France or abroad to interview him, until he died in 1957. And the rue de Lille, where he lived, still hasn't been renamed the rue Maurice Garin."[56]

It's hard now to remember that the Tour de France then wasn't *the* Tour de France as it is now. Then, it was a novelty. It was a novelty that caught on fast, of course, but its winners weren't celebrities in the street. Newspaper photography had a lot to learn and the best that papers could manage were cold, posed photos of the sort you'd get on souvenir postcards. And posed, what's more, on a bicycle so that the often smudged reproduction revealed little of the face. There was no television, remember. And weekly newsreels sent to cinemas were pioneered by Pathé only in 1911. There was a chance to see the stars if you lived near a track, and if the promoters had the money to attract them, but the only hope of seeing a *vedette* apart from that was the chance that one would pass, perhaps in the night, if you lived on the route of a big race from one town to another.

All this starts to explain the odd position that Jean-Marie Jasniewicz and Maurice Vernaldé found themselves in when an Italian television crew turned up at their cemetery on the road between Lens and Sallaumines. Without stopping at the small hut the two occupied to the left of the stone-pillared gates near the cemetery walls, the Italians walked about until they found section F3 and, there, a man-high stone engraved "Familles Brot-Garin et Darnet". Beneath the inscription, in gold on black marble, are five names. The second reads "Maurice Garin 1871–1957". There are two stones in the shape of open bibles but half a century of northern French weather has worn them thin.

Jasniewicz and Vernaldé, the first tall and thoughtful, the other smaller and animated, had tended the graves for fifteen years before the Italians turned up without introducing themselves. When Jasniewicz walked slowly over to see them—cemetery attendants rarely need to hurry—they shamed him by telling what he and Vernaldé had never realised: that they were the guardians of the winner of the first Tour de France.

I went to see them on the day I visited Notre Dame-de-Lorette, a slaughter field of the First World War where more than half a million French troops died in defence of coal mines that the Germans had set their hearts on. There, in the small church, is a small white plaque marking the death of Corporal François Faber, another Tour winner, who died in 1915 while helping an injured colleague out of no man's land. It reads, in capital letters: "François Faber, First Foreign Regiment, winner of the Tour de France cycling race 1909, died for France in May 1915 at Carency." He was in a foreign division because, though he lived in Colombes near Paris, he had been born in Luxembourg.

Lens lies below the ridge. The coal mines that attracted the Germans had been discovered in 1849 by three businessmen from Lille.

The Germans occupied the town almost from the start of the war and what they hadn't destroyed by the end was then knocked down by allied shelling. By 1918 the town was too dangerous to enter, the ruins scattered with unexploded shells. The Germans, before they left, flooded all the mines.

The two caretakers, not having much to do, were quick to join me. "Not many people come", Jasniewicz told me. It was hard to tell if that saddened him or if he was simply acknowledging the fact. He spoke slowly and without emotion, a man who asks no more from life than quiet pride in his job. "Journalists now and again, and quite a few Dutch people for some reason. But maybe only one person a year. Now and again I find flowers here and I don't know who left them. And once a month or so I take a broom to the grave and, out of respect, I sweep round him. But apart from that, he's forgotten, I think."

Vernaldé listened attentively, anxious to join in. When his chance came, it was to say that the town wouldn't even prop up the headstone as it started to sag. "If Garin had been a soccer star or a wartime hero," he said, "we'd have a statue or a plaque. But nobody cares about the winner of the first Tour de France."

In fact, the vélodrome in town was named after him. But that wasn't built until 1933 and, even when it was rebuilt in 1990, nobody thought to rename the street on which it stood. That's still called the avenue Alfred Maës, after a local politician and former miner. And now, after several years of inactivity, the track has been demolished to provide space for a provincial branch of the Louvre museum. Hundreds more came to see the wreckers start work than had watched races in the past decades.

That is now and then was then. It's simply not true that Garin was unknown in Lens when he won. He may have become another confused old man "who loved to tell his stories over and over again", according to Vernaldé, who went to his garage on errands as a boy, but in 1903 he was much the man of the moment. Working from newspaper stories of the day, the French journalist Pierre Chany wrote: "In Maurice Garin's adopted home town of Lens, there was a huge parade with all the notables of the region."[57] It was only afterwards, with his disqualification in 1904, and perhaps because of that, that he became just Citizen Garin.

After the race, of course, Desgrange said he'd known all along that it would succeed. He wasn't so sure before it happened, though. For a start, trips to the mail box in the days following the big announcement were rewarded with little but the everyday correspondence of a daily newspaper. Entries weren't coming in. The limit was 5 p.m. on 15 June, two weeks before the start. Provided a rider could spell his name and address and give the number of his racing license—his membership of a national cycling body—he had only to enclose ten francs if he wanted to ride the whole race, half that for a single day and two for any amateurs who wanted to ride from Toulouse to Bordeaux, along the flat Garonne valley.

Desgrange quietly and privately said that there'd be no Tour unless there were fifty entries, that in reality there would have to be seventy to cover for those who fell ill or just thought better of it before the off. And then, with the entry of the Parisian, Julien Girbe, he had a large enough field. But confidence still didn't brim. If ever there was a day you'd think he'd put nothing but the Tour on his front page, that was the day before the start, the last day of June. But look at the paper now and what do you find? That there's not a word about the Tour de France on the front. It's all given over to the Gordon Bennett Cup, a car race. And a car race, what's more, not in France but in Ireland. Not until the final column of the third page do the organisers mention the race starting next morning. It's headlined "Le Tour de France", in quotation marks that suggest that even the staff didn't feel too confident about the name. And then, in far smaller type, *DEMAIN!* (Tomorrow!).

VOICES FROM THE PAST

We've got the number of entries we wanted and the list isn't yet closed. We were convinced that we would reach the figure of fifty entries that we considered we needed to have a Tour de France. But there were "friends", those whose interest in sport runs only as far as their commercial interest, who delighted that the most beautiful race ever held on the road, the Tour de France, would

> have to be aborted. "What a ridiculous idea!", they wrote. "It will never happen."
>
> —Henri Desgrange takes aim at Pierre Giffard of *Le Vélo*, who first ignored the race and then belittled it.

The crowing, of course, can be seen another way: that it was relief, that all along Desgrange had worried about the coming crash at his feet. *L'Auto* was shouting in public but in private it was still in bad shape. The Tour, remember, had been the only idea worth considering at that emergency meeting. And whether Goddet's gesture with the safe was an act of generosity or cynicism at how little there was to take, the fact is that *L'Auto* was making a hefty loss, that it was heading for extinction, that Desgrange would have to eat humble pie in front of Giffard, while all that time spending vast sums on a race that for a worrying time didn't even have riders to take part.

Once he had them, he could turn once more to the purple ink. "From Paris to the blue waves of the Mediterranean," he oozed, "from Marseille to Bordeaux, passing along the roseate and dreaming fields sleeping under the sun, across the calm fields of the Vendée, following the Loire which flows on still and silent, our men are going to race madly, unflaggingly." It was what Geoffrey Nicholson called "the mandarin style of cycle reporting which has endured to this day".[58]

Desgrange elected to be a general leading from the rear. It may have been a wise move—there was no point in organising the Tour if the paper didn't appear next morning—but it wouldn't be the last time Desgrange stayed home when he worried things could go wrong. He did it again when he first took the Tour through the mountains, turning back to Paris rather than be on the spot at the moment that fate would determine the truth or otherwise of riders' predictions that they'd be eaten by bears.

Instead he sent Georges Abran to Montgeron as starter, a role he combined with the relaxed drinking of pastis, the alcoholic aniseed drink of the peasant south, and Géo Lefèvre to report the race as best he could by bike and then by catching a train to the finish. The colour came from Olivier Margot, who reported of that first day that "the men waved their hats, the ladies their umbrellas. You felt they would have liked to touch the steel muscles of the most courageous champions since Antiquity. Yes, the most courageous because—a revolution in our splendid sport of cycling—the race will be run without pacemakers except on the final stage. And end to the combines and Apaches [a fashionable word at the time for crooks and wide-boys] of every stamp. Only muscles and energy will win glory and fortune."

The riders changed in a cellar beneath the Réveil Matin. There's nothing left of the race down there: it's all been stolen by souvenir-hunters. Only twenty-one of the starters reached the finish. All Desgrange cared was that enough would get back to Paris so that he could get them riding a final race-off on his Parc des Princes. And his only interest in that was that he could sell tickets if there were a decent number, whereas those who watched in the street paid him nothing. That's another reason he allowed riders who'd dropped out one day to start again the next, eligible for prizes at the end of each stage but not for the overall competition, the *classement général*. It kept the show going.

Other than that, it was of only passing interest to him if riders dropped out of his race. Or if they found it horribly hard. The aim was to portray competitors as supermen and to present the winner to an ailing public as an example of how they too could be. The Tour de France was a precursor of those body-building ads that promised to seven-stone weaklings that they would no longer have sand kicked in their faces.[59] Around three out of four riders never made the finish until the late 1920s. Then drop-outs decreased along with the distance of each day's race. From the 1920s the rate dropped from around seventy-five per cent to around half. It is now about twenty per cent.[60] Riders who could survive to the end were the last thing Desgrange wanted. The more who caught the train home, the more they elevated those who remained.

Victor Goddet, still fretting whether he'd done the right thing, drove to the start with his friends Georges Berg and Victor Laborde. Planning had cost *L'Auto* around 40,000 francs, of which a quarter went on the salaries of forty-two employees. Desgrange stared at the riders as they arrived at the paper's offices, trying to recognise them, because they were as unfamiliar to him as everyone else. He wrote of them as though he knew them, though, and he gave them eccentric nicknames such as "the heel-pedaller" and "the blacksmith" to familiarise them to his readers. But he had never seen still less met most of them. So when he deigned to visit his own race, he watched who took which numbers from the registration table run by Alphonse Steinès, who a few years later would be responsible for taking the Tour across the Pyrenees for the first time.

The first to sign on were Henri Ellinamour and Léon Pernette. Both collected green armbands and a number to hang from their bicycle. Outside the bar, Jean Fischer was standing with his bike, with which he'd travelled on the train and then ridden from the nearest station. Beside him were bottles of soup, a spare tyre and chain, but little luggage. He had arranged for a friend to meet him in Lyon at the end of that stage with his suitcase and with 250 francs to help pay his expenses. An itinerant salesman calling himself Boum-Boum and insisting he was from Algeria pressed the crowd to buy more Coco, the fizzy pop of the day. Claude Chapperon and Émile Moulin turned up at the last moment after missing their train.

Reporters were there not just from *L'Auto* but from *L'Éclair, Armes et Sports, La Gironde* and *Le Figaro.* Officials in blue armbands hustled the riders to the start and counted: sixty starters, conforming with Steinès' signing-on sheet. And the whole bunch, now running late, were marshalled the 600 metres to the junction where the race was to start. Nobody wore cycling clothes that we'd recognise now. Most were in variations of everyday working clothes and one or two wore straw hats. A Belgian called Marcel Kerff looked more like an African hunter, dressed in a white explorer's jacket with copious front pockets, pale trousers drawn into socks beneath the knee, and a cap with a large flap at the back to protect his neck from the sun.

And so, at 3:16 in the afternoon, Georges Abran adjusted his white straw boater and took out his revolver. He wore a jacket with a waistcoat and trousers that did not match. With a last look, he fired the revolver and the first Tour de France set off from Montgeron for its *tour*—circuit—of the country. *L'Auto* that morning had told France that "with the broad and powerful swing of the hand which Zola in *The Earth* gave to his ploughman, *L'Auto*, newspaper of ideas and action, is going to fling across France today those reckless and uncouth sowers of energy who are the great professional riders of the road."

What they made of being called reckless and uncouth is your guess but it set from the start the relationship that riders were going to have with the man who deigned to let them take part. It was an attitude that Desgrange perfected year by year until he died in 1940, the year that German troops swept in across France from the north while the British were thinking better of it and fleeing from the beaches of Dunkirk. His dreams of creating an invincible French youth had finally ended.

At the Réveil Matin, the riders set off as the crowd admired "the steel muscles of the most courageous champions since Antiquity." They rode off along the avenue Jean-Jaurès, under the railway bridge, past the cemetery, into the main part of Montgeron, on past the Sénart forest and so towards Lyon 467 kilometres to the south-east, largely following the railway line. They left in the afternoon because they were expected to ride through the night before finishing late the next day. Pedalling among them for a while was Géo Lefèvre, riding and watching until he got to a station where he could catch a train to further along the course and then another to the finish.

Garin finished his day in 17 hours 45 minutes 13 seconds, winning the stage at an average of 26 kilometres per hour, a speed even experienced brevet riders can't always match today, and finished the stage before the judges got there. But as Pierre Chany pointed out, "Until and up to 1927, the advertised distances rarely matched the distance that riders actually rode. Because of that, the official averages were rarely accurate. From 1928, the distances, the time-keeping and the calculation of averages were more rigorous. But even so, it was still the case that the announced distances were not necessarily accurate."[61]

Desgrange didn't stint in his treatment of riders. In Nantes, in the rest days that preceded the final stint to Paris, he put them up in the rue Crébillon, in the grand surroundings of the Hôtel des Voyageurs. It's now called the Hôtel de France after merging with its neighbour. "What a contrast [it must have been]", wrote one commentator, "between these rough, half-starved men pushing their bikes into a hotel with its sculpted cherubs, which these days welcomes the top levels of the arts and politics… [These were] amateurs for the most part, simple men little used to being shown such luxury."[62]

After their days of rest—riders often walked round town or went on bike trips into the countryside (in 1910, Adolphe Helière drowned while swimming, perhaps stung by a jellyfish)—the rough, half-starved men pushed their bikes back out of the hotel and into a square surrounded by elegant stone buildings with arcades at their base. Other than now being a paved area easier for pedestrians than drivers, it doubtless looks little different from that last morning of the first Tour de France.

The wind blew from the west for their eastward journey to the capital. It was 8 p.m. The sun would set in another two hours. The bunch left on the bumpy, stony roads, making good time on the largely flat roads through Ancenis, Angers, Saumur, Blois and Tours, following the Loire and its châteaux. Crowds were there along the road to cheer and wave their hats. One guess had 10,000 in the Place des Armes in Versailles. As night fell, fans and officials who had cars turned on their headlights to light the road.

VOICES FROM THE PAST

The cycling world gives a rider a false glory, with successes on the track, all that delights you, but it masks the sad reality of things. You've seen the great champions carried in triumph and that's all you saw, just as when you were young and at the theatre you saw only the brilliant and charming actresses. Did you look further? Did you see the sad and miserable people in the street, ragged and penniless, the shrivelled old women selling bouquets of violets? They are the invalids of glory: one-time actors, one-time cyclists, one-time music stars. Once they knew popularity; today they're holding out their hand.

—Henri Desgrange in one of his letters to a young rider in *La Tête et les Jambes*, 1895

The ride wasn't without incident. One colourful—overly colourful—story in *La République d'Orléans* insisted that a pig panicked and ran into the bunch. There it felled one of the riders, who tumbled on to its back and clung to its neck as the pig dragged him away in panic. More certain and more tragic is that two motorcyclists who followed the race crashed; one was badly injured and the other died shortly afterwards.

The pig story, by the way, turns up surprisingly often in cycle racing and it's a reminder that reporters from Géo Lefèvre onwards saw little of the races they recounted. They relied on the riders' accounts and on spectators, and sometimes the stories were too good not to use. And so in the Tour of 1920 Napoléon Paoli was said to have hit a donkey on the road to Bayonne and ended up on its back as it galloped away. It stopped only when it hurt its leg. Paoli then let go, ran back for his bike, and continued the race only for a rock to fall from a cliff and hit him on the head. He rode on as far as the foot of the Tourmalet, where the pain became too much and he fell asleep in a hut. He started the Tour in 1919, 1920 and 1921 and finished none of them. The donkey story is the only one known about him and we shouldn't rush to think it is true.

More easily confirmed is that Fernand Augereau ran into a photographer who stepped out to snap the final mass finish in Ville d'Avray and fell on his face. Maurice Garin won that stage, his third, and he accepted the crowd's applause, answered questions, stared at cameras for photos, then entered the Père Auto restaurant. There, with other riders, he had glass of champagne in the garden, washed as best he could, and then half an hour later lined up with the other survivors for the ceremonial ride to the Parc des Princes six kilometres away, each rider setting off according to his position in the race.

The Parc is now a concrete monstrosity surrounded by walls, barbed wire and uniformed guards who politely discourage inquiries. No bike racing goes on there now. It's an international soccer stadium, home to France's biggest team, Paris St-Germain. The bike track was competent for its time, with steep pink bankings, untold numbers of standing places and dated grandstands. It had towards the end, it's true, more romance than practicality, but many an old fan remembers it with rheumy eyes.

Every Tour finished there from 1903 until 1967, by which time half the seats had already been removed. The wreckers waited until Roger Pingeon had made his tour of honour and gone home and then they moved in. Most of it lies now under the Paris ring road, the new stadium having been put up to one side. It went because of a legal oversight. The Tour, which ran it and believed it owned it, was long required to let local children use it during the week. This, argued Paris' politicians, showed the Tour was not the owner but an operator and a tenant. No owner could be compelled to allow children to enter. If that was the case, then Paris was free to evict a tenant and demolish the track.

Jacques Goddet fought the ruling. But he lost and he had to walk away with not a centime in compensation and with no chance to appeal. That, anyway, is Goddet's telling of the story in his autobiography, *L'Equipée Belle*. Robert Lewis, an expert on stadiums, makes it sound less one-sided, that there was "pent-up municipal exasperation at the venerable Jacques Goddet at *L'Équipe* [the paper that succeeded *L'Auto*] and his administrative control." Venerable, probably, in the sense of magisterial rather ancient, because Goddet was sixty-two when the track came down, which was fifteen years younger than Charles de Gaulle, the president and Paris's ultimate administrator in the days before it had a mayor.

Lewis goes on: "The city had long been dissatisfied with the contract that Jacques Goddet's father, Victor Goddet, and his business partner Henri Desgrange had negotiated back in 1924, when their Société Anonyme du Parc des Princes had signed a forty-year lease on the land for the Parc. Municipal frustration stemmed mostly from a sense that Paris was not getting an appropriate cut of the revenue generated by football matches at the stadium, but attempts to revise the contract in the city's favour had proved largely unsuccessful over the decades. Thus the municipal council refused to renew the Parc's lease in 1963, mostly in hope of resolving a long-standing fiscal irritation."[63]

Even then the Tour wouldn't budge. You can imagine the frustration of dealing with Jacques Goddet and, at the same time, the pressing need to build a ring road. What had been a city of horses in the days of the Michaux family now had 1,700,000 cars for 330,000 parking spaces.[64] Traffic blocked the streets. Paris needed a bypass and, like many cities, it was in the thrall of concreting and had a belief in the godlike superiority, the need, of the petrol engine. Which has its irony, given that *L'Auto* had been so named because it saw motoring as the future. Paris abandoned its first idea, which was to take a tunnel under the track, and it decided it would rather demolish one of its own buildings and remove the inconvenience—not to mention ending the long-running irritation of dealing with first Desgrange and then Goddet.

Laws required it to replace one stadium by another and so Paris designed the new football stadium. It was decried as a dreadful waste of money and the French cycling federation and, predictably, *L'Équipe* did all they could to protest and to shout that there was no plan to include a bike track. The best that Paris had was the 1900 Olympic Games track at Vincennes,[65] which is where the Tour decamped until it persuaded a fresh Paris administration to give it the Champs Elysées. But down came the old track in the Parc, the demolition carried out by the Bouygues company that later sponsored a professional road team that itself rode the Tour de France. It took five years to build the new stadium.

That day back in 1903, the old stadium was close to full. Garin was led through the track tunnel in the white jersey by which he was recognised—there was as yet no yellow jersey for the leader—but now wearing a blue, white and red sash over his right shoulder. A small boy came to take his bike and officials prepared to shoo him away. Garin intervened: "It's my son", he said.

Géo Lefèvre wrote: "France for three weeks has been encircled by enthusiasm: at night I saw countrymen emerge from their cottages to light beacons of joy in honour of the speeding phantoms… I saw peaceful towns turned into a fever by this savage battle that they had never imagined the day before; I saw the uninitiated conquered by that of which they would never have known had we not made them spectators at a great battle of the road... I heard them say 'Next year, we will ride the Tour de France!'"

5
Looking for a superman

There was a period at the end of the nineteenth century when many serious-minded people believed in social Darwinism. The argument was that Charles Darwin had established that success in the animal world went to the strongest, that winners passed on their genes and that their race strengthened as a result. If that was the case, social Darwinists argued, why should it not also apply to humans? Darwin himself certainly thought so, writing that vaccinating against smallpox kept alive those who would make humans stronger by their death.

The root of the argument obviously had some weight. But, working from that, many went further and argued that the weak—defined by those who thought themselves strong and therefore exempt from the consequences—should be forbidden to have children and, at the extremes of the argument, that they should be killed. The Nazi death camps were the execution of this theory at its extreme but it was practised elsewhere. Gerard Oram's military history, *Worthless Men,* explains how British army courts trying soldiers for desertion in the First World War occasionally decided against the soldier in case of doubt because the world would be better off without a "worthless man".[66] Sweden and the United States both sterilised women they believed mentally weak.

Now, there's no evidence that Desgrange was a believer, although he could not have avoided knowing the theory because he and it were of the same period. But there is, nevertheless, that belief that French youth had become weak-bodied and weak-willed, that France was no longer the great war-winning nation that it had been in Napoleon's time, and that something should be done about it. He wrote in the first issue of *L'Auto* that, thanks to sport and the backing that his paper would give it, "our race will soon find itself radically transformed", but there was no explanation of just what he meant by "race." It could, of course, have meant simply the human race but social Darwinism was at the time also being used to justify the domination and colonisation of black men.

VOICES FROM THE PAST

With savages, the weak in body or mind are soon eliminated; and those that survive commonly exhibit a vigorous state of health. We civilised men, on the other hand, do our utmost to check the process of elimination; we build asylums for the imbecile, the maimed, and the sick; we institute poor-laws; and our medical men exert their utmost skill to save the life of every one to the last moment. There is reason to believe that vaccination has preserved thousands, who from a weak constitution would formerly have succumbed to small-pox. Thus the weak members of civilised societies propagate their kind. No one who has attended to the breeding of domestic animals will doubt that this must be highly injurious to the race of man.

—Charles Darwin, *The Descent of Man*

Desgrange, thankfully, looked at the problem in the other direction: to find and then promote a superman, a superior being who by example would inspire other young people and lead them out of inferiority—of which he was to be the judge—and on to national glory. It is not easy to work out his politics. He refused political comment in *L'Auto* not because he was apolitical—it's hard to think that anyone so dogmatic could not have firm beliefs—but for the practical commercial reason that he had seen politics sink *Le Vélo* and he had no interest in putting himself on the chopping block in the same way.

His instant disqualification of riders who displeased him—such as Maurice Brocco who, having no further chance himself, sold his services to others—and the way he simply overruled judges' decisions when he chose, portrays an absolute ruler, perhaps a dictator. As Geoffrey Wheatcroft put it, he had a dictatorial manner with a "habit of arbitrarily, and often foolishly, changing the rules before a Tour began or even when it was in progress, his astonishing capacity for abusing riders in print."[67] He had been an anti-Dreyfusard in the 1890s, Wheatcroft adds without offering evidence, "and he was no simpering liberal ever after."

You'd think, then, that he was of the right. And certainly, as we've seen, he was quick to hold up historical figures, particularly Napoleon, as illustrations in his writing. It's certainly unlikely he was of the left. But the way he actually leaned remains a mystery. Except that…

Except that Desgrange in May 1901 engaged the sprinter, Marshall Taylor, to race against the French idol, Edmond Jacquelin, at the Parc des Princes. Jacquelin, a handsome, clean-cut man, was seen as and took himself to be the royalty of the track. According to Pierre Chany, working from newspapers of the period, Jacquelin was a charmer, a raconteur, a lady's man who could hold his table spellbound at the most chic of restaurants.

Taylor, on the other hand, was a serious, Bible-carrying man, one of eight born to a black family on a farm near Indianapolis in central USA. To make money as a boy he performed cycling stunts outside a bike shop in the city, dressed in military uniform. Because of the uniform he became known as Major, a nickname that stuck. When he grew, he became cycling's first black world champion. The League of American Wheelmen, the governing body, had got round to letting black riders join but it would not let them race. Going to Europe, then, was an escape from racism at home. And that is how he came to ride on the Parc des Princes.

Now, it has to be said that racism also existed in France, but it was a lot less obvious than in America. Black men, perhaps because of their scarcity—France had black colonies and still has black *départements*, but those who lived there came only in small numbers to the country's heartland—were sometimes adopted almost as public pets. And that was how it was for Taylor in Paris, liked by the crowd. Desgrange was no fool: he knew the emotions and therefore the chance to sell tickets would be fanned by pitching a black foreigner, however liked, against a white god. Taylor was sure to have played along to some extent because he too depended for his living on ticket sales. And the sales were helped by this being a revenge match, Taylor having finished second to Jacquelin the previous week.

On the day of the re-match, Desgrange pocketed the turnstile takings, and he clearly hoped that his Frenchman would win. He didn't, and legend says that Desgrange exercised his spite by paying Taylor his prizes in the ten-centime coins recovered from the pay counters. Legend says that Taylor needed a wheelbarrow to cart them away.

It *could* have been, of course, that Jacquelin would also have been paid that way, in small coins, though it seems improbable. It could also be that the story simply isn't true. It's probably not, because the reported first prize was $7,500. In 1901, France adhered to the gold standard, which kept the franc at a constant value to the dollar. There were 5.18 francs to the US dollar so Taylor won 38,850 francs. Paid 10 centimes at a time, that meant 388,500 coins. How many coins to a wheelbarrow? Perhaps he made several trips but, frankly, the probability meter doesn't twitch, does it?

Search for "Taylor-Jacquelin-*brouette*"[68] on the internet and you get nothing. Like the bare calves story and the woman who cost Desgrange his job, the incident is better known outside France than inside. It's repeated in Marlene Targ Brill's book,[69] it's told again by Daniel de Visé.[70] It's told everywhere. Except in France, at least on the internet, where it's supposed to have happened.

Maybe it's more likely that someone laughed that "he probably needed a wheelbarrow to cart it away" and that a joking remark spread as fact. But the fact that it's told suggests that it illustrates Desgrange's view of life.

Little went right in Taylor's life when he stopped cycling, by the way. He was a rich man but he put his money into business ventures which failed. Some he invested in shares, only to be wiped out by the stock-market crash. His house and much of what he owned was sold to cover the debts. He became ill and tried to survive by knocking on doors to sell his life story, a book he had himself published but which seems never to have covered its costs. He died aged fifty-three and was buried in an unmarked pauper's grave. No one claimed his remains and nobody thought to tell his wife and daughter.

Sixteen years later, the Schwinn bicycle company put up the money to have him exhumed and placed in a more prominent part of the cemetery, where his memorial reads "Dedicated to the memory of Marshall W. 'Major' Taylor, 1878–1932. World's champion bicycle racer who came up the hard way without hatred in his heart, an honest, courageous and god-fearing, clean-living, gentlemanly athlete. A credit to the race who always gave out his best. Gone but not forgotten."

VOICES FROM THE PAST

> The moral turpitude of the boys of today appears to centre in their failure to concentrate on any particular objective long enough to obtain their maximum results.
>
> —Major Taylor

Desgrange's desire for a superman, preferably French, involved not just pride in his country but a nationalism that matched the tone of the era. This, remember, was a time when Johnny Foreigner was suspected until, to general surprise, he proved himself honest. Otherwise he was automatically shifty, or at best comical, our side trustworthy, honest and reasonable, theirs given to silly feathered helmets and copious awards with ridiculous names. Germans were argumentative, the British devious, the Italians excitable and the French just awkward. It offended national pride when they won and we lost.

France had lost some of its north-eastern territory to Germany in the final conflict of the Franco-Prussian war that was so strong in Desgrange's mind. To make a point that France lived on despite her disgrace, and that the Tour was a virile symbol of that continuity, Desgrange planned in 1906 to take his race through the lost territories. He went so far out of his way, literally, that the Tour was 1,600 kilometres longer than the year before.

He went through the usual formal channels to ask the German governor in Strasbourg for permission to use the crossing east of Longwy. Either the governor saw things the other way round from Desgrange—that asking permission to ride in countryside that was once French confirmed that France was a supplicant to German superiority—or, looked at cheerfully, he decided the war was gone and that he wanted Germany and France to accept the position and be friends. Either way, he asked his bosses in Berlin and they telegraphed back that they agreed.

This was the first time the race had left France and, so far as we know, it could have been one of the first times that Desgrange himself had left France, especially into the land of the enemy. On 9 May 1906, he wrote again to propose to the German governor that "every rider and his racing bicycle may enter Alsace-Lorraine without paying a border charge, should there be one" The letter is now in the Moselle regional archives.

The people in the captured areas now within Germany still thought of themselves as French. Victor Breyer, the thin-faced, British-born assistant organiser of the Tour,[71] wrote of the Tour's arrival that local people cheered the riders and even French cars. The Germans, he said, were polite and helpful and the police made no effort to stop speeding drivers. "You'd never get that from a French policeman", he wrote.

Things went well all through Germany, neither side wanting to appear less than perfect in the eyes of the other. But Desgrange's desire to show France as a land of culture, learning and sporting success collapsed when the Tour came to the border to cross back into its home country. The Germans, a reporter wrote, were *minutieuses* (meticulous), smart and polite. It was a hundred metres further on, at the entry to France, that things went wrong.

"Woken from a deep sleep, obliged to get up in three minutes, the German customs men appeared before us in new uniforms", France learned next morning. "At the French border, by contrast, it was simply distressing. Smelly, covered in mud, their clothes patched and discoloured, backs bent, squashed kepis on dirty bodies, the two officials charged with nosing around on behalf of the tax authorities and who represented France revolted us."

They took so long doing it that Breyer had to organise a second start. *L'Auto*, with despairing irony, impertinently "but very seriously" later proposed it should open a public appeal to dress its frontier staff decently.

Desgrange repeated the incursions over the years, visiting Metz and being greeted by the splendidly bald and moustachioed Count Zeppelin. We're going back far enough now that Ferdinand von Zeppelin had been an observer at the American civil war. It was there that he learned about balloons and had his first experience beneath one. Six years before the Tour visited his fiefdom in Metz, he had flown one of his own airships over Lake Constance in southern Germany. Seven years later, the man who had smiled at the Tour de France was instrumental in the balloon bombing of Allied cities in the First World War.

Relations between the men soured. Nobody then doubted that there would be a war.

> VOICES FROM THE PAST
>
> I have to admit that I am not happy. I have now been to Metz twice. Last year, in July, at the finish of the Tour de France, you were absent. This time, for the organisation, I did not have the honour of meeting you. I can only regret that, used as I am to being so well received and above all in such a friendly way. I hope I will be happier in July, on the fifth, and that you will do us the honour of adding to the lustre of the occasion by your presence at the finish, accompanied by your charming wife, the Countess Zeppelin. I still remember well the pleasure you gave us three years ago, joined by Madame the Countess, when the riders crossed the line.
>
> —Henri Desgrange upbraids Zeppelin for not taking the Tour sufficiently seriously, 18 April 1910.

War broke out on 28 July 1914. As a not inconsiderable aside, the day the 1914 Tour started was the day that Franz Ferdinand was assassinated in Sarajevo. The falling house of cards that led to war happened while the race was on the road. The Tour finished on 26 July; the riders and officials had only just got home when the war began. Desgrange broke his rule of having no politics in his paper and wrote an editorial column of sickening blood-thirstiness.

"My boys! My dear boys! My dear young boys of France! Listen to me. The Prussians are bastards. You've got to get them. And you've got to do it straight away because if you don't get them, they'll have you. And when you get them... [and] you have your gun against their chest, they will beg you to spare them. Don't do it. Drive in your bayonet without pity. You need to get rid of these wicked imbeciles who, for forty years, have forbidden us to live, to love, to breathe and be happy. Ah, how the whole of humanity will sigh, my dear boys, if you are victorious. How we shall breathe! How we'll find life good and beautiful… There'll be no more Kaiser! No more Agadir![72] No more blood tax! No more nightmares! No more bastards! We won the first round at Jena and they won the next in Sedan.[73] Now for us the best of three if you want it, as only French people can want things."

His wish? That "they will understand that [the confiscated provinces of] Alsace and Lorraine are French!"

There was much more. It filled the first column and a half of the first page, under the headline "*Le grand match*", a sporting trivialisation of a war we know now, but he didn't know then, would last more than four years and kill millions. Again there was that sporting reference in the best of three, with France winning *la belle*, the play-off.

There is much in that that now embarrasses. Then, it was a hyperbolic tone that Desgrange's readers would have known and which made his paper the market leader. And it is always a mistake to sit in the present and judge the attitudes and actions of the past. It would be easy to dismiss Desgrange as a bad-tempered old man eager to send boys into battle and save France with their blood rather than his. But he could surprise. At fifty-three, he volunteered for the twenty-ninth infantry regiment at Autun in 1917. There he wore his ribbon of the Légion d'honneur, awarded in December, 1904, and wrote dispatches for *L'Auto* as Henri Desgrenier ("of the attic" rather than the "of the barn" of Desgrange). He was made an officer in May 1919.

By the time the war ended, some of cycling's greatest names were dead.

You can't go far in France without noticing the war memorials. Every village has one. Weeping angels, sobbing mothers or wives, crouch beside the fallen. Sometimes a *poilu* is shown proud in his pale blue uniform, his body encircled by bags and pouches. He inevitably has a moustache and he often carries a rifle. Often, the rifle is a real one. Untold numbers were left over when silence fell on the trenches in November, 1918, and this being a war to end all wars, there would be no further use for them. It was cheaper and faster to use a real rifle than sculpt one for a memorial and so, across France, stone soldiers peer endlessly into the distance with a real gun at their sides.

Of the 4,830,000 who died in the allied armies between 1914 and 1918, no fewer than 1,150,000 were French. This isn't a competition but the whole British Empire combined lost 953,000. In all, including civilians, French losses have been put at 1,400,000. And that in a nation of forty-one million. Not until 1950 did the population of France return to what it had been in 1914.[74]

When cyclists speak now of the Hell of the North, they take it as a reference to the particularly bad roads chosen for Paris–Roubaix. You understand what it really means when you see it in the original French, in which "north" is given as Nord. The Nord is an administrative area of France, the one in which much of the fighting took place on the western front. Little still stood. Communications no longer existed. People drank water poisoned by the rotting bodies and the toxic munitions that polluted the rivers. They lived in the houses left wrecked, sometimes roofless or missing one wall, that were all that remained when the guns stopped.

It was that that Eugène Christophe saw—he'll return to our story later because, for the moment, we're jumping ahead of ourselves—when he joined organisers as they drove north to see whether they could revive Paris–Roubaix, to see if Roubaix even still existed. Christophe was there to supply the rider's angle, to add colour. And on the return journey he coined a term that has never been forgotten even if now it's misused. He said: "*Nous avons vu l'enfer du Nord*"—we have seen the hell of the North. Capital N, reference to a specific region and not, as often used now, shorthand for the bad roads for which Paris–Roubaix looks out in northern France.

The 1919 Tour had barely started when the war formally ended with France and Germany signing the Treaty of Versailles. The Germans' train was deliberately taken on a longer route so that they would see the devastation attributed to them and which they were about to find they were expected to pay.

There are many differences between the Tour of now and then. Now, the most popular stages on television are those in the mountains. The French public broadcaster, France 2, from which stations around the world take their pictures, starts broadcasting before the riders have left and stays with them well beyond the finish. Every blow is shown and then, after the finish, discussed and analysed. On the mountains themselves, the roadside is occupied from days before the riders pass by a cacophony of French, Dutch and Belgian fans, and sometimes those from elsewhere, passing the time outside their motor-homes with barbecue spits and a more than adequate supply of beer and wine. By the time the riders arrive, a community has established itself and friendships have been made. And a lot of drink has been sunk.

In those early days, though, nobody went into the mountains. There were strange, uncommunicative men there who sat with their sheep, fiercely suspicious and introverted, usually illiterate. But other than that, nobody went. There weren't even roads. Alan Gayfer, the editor of *Cycling* in the 1960s, told of the day he was on a pass in the Pyrenees when he fell into conversation with an elderly man also waiting for the riders.

"We chatted for a while and then, rather shyly, he said he'd ridden the Tour de France forty years earlier. Well, that was in the 1960s, so it'd have been the '20s. I said the roads must have been very different, and he said '*Oui monsieur*, they were very rough surfaces then.' I pointed at the way the riders would be coming and said I'd seen the climb in the days of [Louison] Bobet and [Fausto] Coppi, when there were holes in the surface and stones and rocks on the road. Now, of course, they're in a very good state, more or less smooth like any other road. And he looked very surprised and he said '*Non monsieur*, you don't understand. We didn't come up there!' And he turned and pointed at a tiny goat track behind us, all rocks and tufts of grass and no more than a few yards wide. 'We came up *that road*, there!'"[75]

It's only when you know that, and that there were bears in the mountains, and that tremendous storms could suddenly break there, when you realise how awful was the prospect of crossing the mountains, that you realise just how much Desgrange hoped to find a superman. Riders were used to roads they had never previously seen, and visiting towns that had been only names. But *nobody* had been in the mountains. They were a terrifying prospect. Even Desgrange was concerned. And when it came to it, he had diplomatic flu and stayed away.

In the back of his mind must have been the day in 1905 when he included the Ballon d'Alsace, a great humpty-backed mountain in the north-east near Mulhouse. The Tour had already been up the col de la

République, near St-Étienne, where rifles and bicycles were made, but by comparison that was just a hill. The Ballon at 1,247 metres was only slightly higher than the République but quite different. It often rained, the wind blew and snow made it impassable much of the year.

Desgrange had boasted that nobody could ride the Ballon. Nobody, perhaps he hoped, but a true superman. And that year Desgrange found one when René Pottier not only rode all the way without stopping but, the following year, overtook Desgrange's car. He once had such a lead on more humble riders that he sat in a bar with a jug of wine to wait for them, then beat them into Nice by twenty-six minutes.

He sounds a joker, a great laugh. But he was anything but. He rarely smiled, hardly spoke. His mouth below a wide moustache was always turned down. On 25 January 1907, he was found hanging from a hook at the Peugeot headquarters in Levallois-Perret, a north-western suburb of Paris. He left no note but his brother blamed "sentimental reasons", which many thought meant his wife had had an affair and left him during the Tour.

Desgrange was torn between excess and fear. The Pyrenees were a wholly different proposition. The idea to go there came from Adolphe Steinès (born in Ahn, Luxembourg, in 1873 as Johann Stenges),[76] whom we last saw when he was signing on riders at Montgeron before the first Tour in 1903. He nagged and nagged until Desgrange didn't quite accept the Pyrenees but—perhaps to shut him up—accepted that Steinès should get out of the office and out of his chair and make the 700 kilometre journey south, close to the Spanish border.

In later life Steinès was a jovial-looking, round-faced man with circular spectacles and an air of good living. And we know his version of what happened in his scouting mission because we have his own account of it.[77]

Steinès knew the area. This self-confessed perpetual cycle-tourist had ridden a bike and driven a car there. He went to Pau. Forty kilometres upstream on the river Gave de Pau is the religious centre of Lourdes where the Virgin Mary is said to have led the peasant Bernadette Soubirous to the healing springs of the Grotte de Massabielle in 1858. If you cross the river in Pau and go the same distance due south, you reach a road junction at Laruns. From there the D918 wiggles east through Eaux-Bonnes and up over the col d'Aubisque.

There, Steinés called on a man called Blanchet, the local head of bridges and roads. He told him he planned to bring the Tour his way. Blanchet said the staff of *L'Auto* must have gone mad.

"Do you *know* the Aubisque?" he demanded.

"Of course," said Steinès airily. "I've just been up there. It's obvious that in the state it's in now, the Tour couldn't go there. But you're going to arrange it."

"Me? But I haven't got a penny for that."

"How much do you think it would cost?"

Blanchet guessed 5,000 francs. Steinès put in a call to Desgrange, something which in those days could take an hour to connect. Blanchet picked up the extension and they heard Desgrange gasp: "Five thousand francs? But you're mad! You want to ruin us? I'll give you 1,500, not a centime more."

"Excellent," Steinès said, exploiting the crackly line. "Did you say 2,000?"

Blanchet insisted the job couldn't be done for less than 5,000. Steinès winked and said he'd find the rest "in an old drawer somewhere."

The road over the Aubisque leads nowhere in particular and then rises to the col de Soulor before dropping to Argelès-Gazost. From there you can go up the valley to where the road narrows at Luz-St-Sauveur. That leads to one of the two climbs of the Tourmalet, the highest pass on the French side of the mountains. Snow fell on it in winter. Steinès couldn't cross it so early in the year and so he returned to Paris and came back a month before the Tour. He went into Sainte-Marie-de-Campan, where years later Christophe mended his forks, ate at the inn opposite the church and got the landlady to find him a driver, a man called Dupont from nearby Bagnères-de-Bigorre. Local knowledge would be essential.

The Tourmalet is nineteen kilometres long and hard. Most of the way up is where the hideous ski resort of La Mongie now stands. It was there that Dupont's car stuck in the snow. The two got out and began to walk but Dupont turned back after 600 metres.

"Bears come over from Spain when it snows," he shouted. "It's six o'clock. It'll be dark soon. I'm not going any further." He told Steinès to look out for the four-metre poles stuck in the snow in the middle of the track.

"Wait for me in Barèges," Steinès called back, referring to the far side of the mountain where the river Bastan bursts through the village at its foot. Dupont reversed and disappeared. Steinès set off into the snow and gloom. He was alone. He heard voices. He was about to be robbed, perhaps killed. But they turned out to be youngsters watching sheep with their dog. Steinès called to one.

"Son, do you know the Tourmalet well?"

"Certainly."

"Could you guide me?"

"Well…"

"I'll give you twenty francs and a gold coin. When we get to the top, I'll give you another one."

"I don't need money."

"Everyone needs money."

"No, I don't. But I'll take you anyway."

The two kilometres to the summit took two and a half hours. Clouds blocked the moon. The road was black. The boy insisted on going back to his sheep. Steinès feared going further alone on an indistinct track, beside threatening precipices. He sat on a rock to wait for dawn, then realised he'd freeze before he it came. He set off again, his legs stiff from the cold, slipping on the icy road. He stumbled into a stream, climbed back to the road and fell again in the snow. Exhausted now and stumbling, he heard a challenge.

"Who's that?"

Steinès didn't answer. Who knew who it might be high on the mountain at night?

"Tell me who goes there or I'll shoot," came the voice.

"I'm a lost traveller. I've just come across the Tourmalet."

The tone changed. "Oh, it's you, Monsieur Steinès! We were expecting you!"

"How do you mean?"

"We got a phone call at Sainte-Marie-de-Campan. Everybody's at Barèges. It's coming on for three o'clock. There are search teams of guides out looking for you."

Barèges was still awake. *L'Auto* had a correspondent there, a man called Lanne-Camy, and he came forward to meet the soaked, shivering and exhausted traveller. "My dear Steinès, what a state you're in!"

he said with understatement. He took him for a hot bath and provided new clothes, too large but welcome.

"I promised to telegram Desgrange," Steinès told him once he'd warmed up and changed.

"What are you going to wire?"

"*Je ne sais pas. Ah! Tant pis! A la grâce de Dieu…*" (I don't know. Oh, heck… may God save me…)

"Henri Desgrange, *L'Auto*, Paris," he wrote. "Crossed Tourmalet stop. Very good road stop. Perfectly feasible."

In creating a chase for supermen, Desgrange had revealed a commercial weakness in his race. For the more that mere humans were attracted to vie for the title, the more often they came from abroad. And for all that Desgrange enjoyed showing and then exploiting the borders of France and Frenchness, the truth was that people on one side of an arbitrary line are likely to be no different from those on the other. Since sport is the ultimate capitalist pursuit in which the stronger grind the weaker to obscurity for their own benefit, it began to hurt when foreigners more and more dominated the Tour. It hurt not just patriotically but financially. The French may have pretended that they didn't care who won provided it was done gloriously, their disdain for foreigners showed when they stopped buying *L'Auto*. Frenchmen sold newspapers but foreigners didn't.

Desgrange tinkered with the formula of the race but never again did he get the sales that he had in the 1920s.[78] And his troubles were deepened by Europe's difficult recovery after the world war. Before it and immediately afterwards, French bicycles had sold in France and Belgian bicycles in Belgium, and so on. They each had riders and sometimes even teams to promote them. But so wrecked was French industry in general after 1918 that the few bike companies that had made it that far combined to run a single team between them rather than allow the death of a sport on which they all depended for publicity and therefore sales.

There were still tax charges at national borders in the late 1920s but international sales nevertheless became easier, especially between France and Belgium, which shared a language. French industrialists, sensing they had got as much out of the home market as they could, and unable to hire French stars able to bring them a Tour victory that would balance their books for the year, increasingly turned to Belgians. Belgium was happy to supply them because it had no bike factories worthy of a team.

The man who personified that was a Belgian called Odilon Franciscus Defraye, whose parents Camiel and Sidonie lived in Rumbeke. Then it was in the country and the couple were as poor as anyone else who lived there. Now it is a suburb of Roeselare, or Roulers as it's known in French. Camiel and Sidonie either weren't good at spelling or those they dealt with weren't because their name is given in some early accounts as *Defraeye*, which reflected the local pronunciation of *De-fraya*. History, however, has settled on Defraye and the son's name as Odile (the suffix *-on* is a diminutive in French).

Odile was born on 14 July 1888, and grew to be a square-faced youth with a moustache and with a parting down the centre of his hair. He worked at a broom factory in Izegem and his boss, a man called Vanderkerckhove, got him making deliveries on his bike. Legend says Odile would sometimes make round trips of 200 kilometres, although that sounds unlikely with one broom let alone several and in an era when factories sold mainly to their immediate surroundings. Come what may, the deliveries added to the training that he did and he began winning race after race. But don't get too carried away. According to the Belgian race historian, Rik Vanwalleghem, whom you'll meet if you go to the Tour of Flanders museum in Oudenaarde, there were just 125 licensed racers in Flanders (the northern, Dutch-speaking half of the country) in 1907 and half a dozen tracks, none of them in wonderful condition.

Defraye won the amateur Tour of Flanders and faced a choice. He could continue as an amateur without any slope left to climb, or he could stop cycling, or he could ride for a living. He chose to ride for a living, judging that it if nothing else it would be more fun than delivering brooms. He turned professional in 1909 and, while that didn't absolve him of doing his national service, the army recognised his talent and let him ride the Tour de France that same year.

The standard was higher and being marched about in the army and given things to learn meant he hadn't ridden as much. So he didn't finish. But with the army behind him, he moved south across the border in 1912 and joined Alcyon, one of the top teams of the day, and wore its pale blue jersey. The man in charge of Alcyon was Edmond Gentil, who one by one bought all the other big cycling factories of the day. He bought so many that in 1927 he sponsored no fewer than four teams in the Tour: Alcyon, Thomann, Armor and Labor were all his.

He thought this strange Belgian who spoke little French was out of place in his Tour team. Apart from anything else, he would be a menace with his irresponsible eccentricity. Defraye once won Milan–San Remo and that night sat up playing cards and lost every coin he'd pocketed. And so Defraye would have been sulking at home as his mates went to Paris for the Tour in 1912 were it not that Gentil got an irate call from his sales agent in western Belgium. We know little of the agent other than that his name was Bonte and that he was very cross. "My job is hard enough already, selling your bikes with customs charges," he told Gentil and Ludo Feuillet, the team's manager for the past two years.[79] "Do you intend to make it still harder for me by leaving your star Belgian at home?"

Gentil had no wish to make Bonte's job intolerable or to lose him to another factory. So he said he would include Defraye provided he rode not for himself but for the stick-thin Parisian, Gustave Garrigou. Desgrange's rules insisted that even riders of the same team shouldn't cooperate but everyone knew that it happened when photographers weren't around. Defraye stuck to the agreement and helped Garrigou until it became obvious that further aid was pointless. Garrigou was not going to win the Tour but there was a good chance that Defraye could. So he won it. Bonte, the regional sales man, said "I told you so" and 10,000 people lined Roeselare when Defraye got home.

Suddenly there were bike racers everywhere in Belgium, and races too. Flanders got a daily paper to match *L'Auto* (it was called *Sportwereld*) and soon the birth of the professional Tour of Flanders. Defraye had inspired a nation, or at any rate a province, and he had changed the Tour. After Defraye in 1912, Belgians won the following six Tours, a span that would have been greater had world war not broken out.

Desgrange had to come to terms with the falling popularity of his race at home, some of it caused by the Belgians. Pride was part of it, of course—if the race declined, so too did his new and appealing standing as a giant of the sport—but there was also the matter of money. The changes and frankly, it has to be said, the often ridiculous changes he made—of which the oddest, in retrospect, was to run the race for the most part as a team time-trial—were never allowed to lessen the essential motive: that riders should suffer, because supermen were not produced by cosseting.

However pointless, however little it achieved, suffering for its own sake was spiritually and physically a good thing. The philosopher, Georges Vigarello, looking back at the sixty years he'd known the Tour, recalled: "They even raced during the night. The Tour was a challenge, a madness that forced the inhuman on to humans, something impossible but existing."[80] Sometimes the silliest rows, the most petty of rules, could flare into moments we now recognise as historic. In 1924, for instance, one of the journalists on the race was Albert Londres, a writer rather than a reporter, a giant of his trade who had exposed the evils of prison camps such as Devil's Island.

It's worth remembering that naiveté and opportunity could well have combined in the story that follows. Londres was an innocent in cycling and the riders concerned knew not only that, but also that one of them, Henri Pélissier, was a disagreeable schemer largely without friends. When, as a result of this story, he tried to found a riders' trade union, most refused to join not because they were against the idea but because they couldn't tolerate being represented by someone so unpleasant. In 1927, then, Albert Londres had been commissioned by *Le Petit Parisien* and our story finds him on the road between Cherbourg and Brest.[81]

> That morning, we had gone ahead of the race. Six o'clock was sounding when we reached Granville. Riders suddenly began sweeping by. And the crowd, convinced by what they were doing, shouted "Henri! Francis!"
>
> Henri and Francis [Pélissier] weren't there. We waited. The shadows passed—the shadows were the *touristes-routiers*, brave little lads who didn't belong to the rich bike factories, who didn't have guts so much in their stomach as their heart. Neither Henri nor Francis turned up. The news came: the Pélissiers had given up. We went back to our Renault and, without a thought for the tyres, we went back up to Cherbourg. The Pélissiers were worth more than a set of tyres. At Coutances, a couple of kids were talking.

"Have you seen the Pélissiers?"

"I could have reached out and touched them", one of them answered.

"You know where they are?"

"At a bar at the station. Everyone's there."

And a whole crowd *was* there. We had to elbow our way into the bistro. The crowd was silent. Nobody was talking but they were looking, open-mouthed, towards the back of the room. Three racing jerseys were installed in front of three bowls of hot chocolate. There were Henri and Francis and the third was none other than the second, Ville—who had finished second at Le Havre and Cherbourg.

"Got problems?" [*Un coup de tête?*]

"No", Henry says. "But we're not dogs."

"What's happened?"

"*Question de bottes.*[82] Or more precisely, a matter of jerseys. This morning in Cherbourg, a race referee came up to me and, without even saying anything, lifted my jersey. He wanted to be sure I didn't have two on. What would *you* say if I pulled up your jacket to see if your shirt was white? I just didn't like his manners."

"What did it have to do with him if you had two jerseys?"

"I could have had fifteen jerseys, but I wasn't allowed to set off with two jerseys but get to the finish in only one."

"Why?"

"It's the rules. We have to race like animals and freeze and suffer in the heat. That's racing, it seems. So I went to find Desgrange. I said, 'So I can't throw off a jersey on the road, then?'"

"No, you can't throw away the Tour's jerseys."

"It's not the Tour's jersey. It's mine."

"I'm not going to discuss this in the road."

"If you won't discuss it in the road, I'm going back to bed."

"We can sort this all out in Brest."

"Yes, that'll all be sorted by Brest because I'm packing it in. And I packed it in."

"And your brother?"

Dirty Feet

"My brother's my brother, isn't that right, Francis?" They embrace each other over their chocolate. "Francis was still riding. I went up to him in the peloton and I said 'Come on, Francis! We're chucking it in.'"

"And that suited me [*cela tombait comme du beurre frais sur une tartine*[83]]", Francis says. "To tell the truth, I had stomach ache this morning and I wasn't keen to be racing."

"And you, Ville?"

"Me?", Ville said, laughing like a baby. "They found me in trouble on the road. I was having troubles with my knees [*les rotules en os de mort*]."

The Pélissiers didn't just have strong legs; they had brains as well.

"You've no idea what the Tour is like", Henri says. "It's a Calvary. But the road to the cross only had twelve stations: we have fifteen.[84] We suffer from the start to the finish. And you want to know how we cope? Look..." He gets a phial from his bag. "That's cocaine for my eyes, and that's chloroform for my gums."

"That," says Ville as he empties his own bag, "that's something to keep my knees warm."

"Pills? You want to see pills? Here you are... pills!" They each get out three boxes.

"And there you are", says Francis. "We ride on dynamite."

Henri replies: "You haven't seen us in the bath at the finish. Come and see. Once we've got the mud off, we're as white as shrouds. We're emptied out by diarrhœa. We faint in the water. In the evening, in our room, we have St Vitus's dance. We can't sleep. Look... our shoe laces are made of leather but even they snap sometimes, even though I suppose they're made of tanned leather. So think what happens to our skin! We're so thin that we slide through our socks, through our shorts, because there's nothing left of us."

"Our flesh no longer sticks to our bones", Francis says.

"And our toenails," Henri says. "I've lost six of the ten. They fall off little by little with each stage."

"But they grow again ready for the next year", says Francis.

The two brothers embrace other again across their chocolate.

"But all that's nothing. Wait until the Pyrenees. That's hard labour. We can put up with that. What they wouldn't make a mule do, we can do. We're not slackers. But in the name of God, don't pile it on. We don't need torment, we don't need abuse. I'm Pélissier, not a dog. If I put a newspaper up my jersey [as insulation] at the start, it still has to be there at the finish. Throw it away and I get penalised. If we're dying of thirst, before we risk taking water, we have to check that there's no one fifty metres away somehow working the pump. Otherwise a penalty, because we have to do the pumping ourselves if we want to drink.

"The day will come when they'll want to put lead in our pockets because they'll decide that God has made men too light. Carry on like that and soon there'll be just tramps and no artists.[85] The sport's going crazy."

"Yes", says Ville. "Crazy."

A kid comes up to us.

"What do you want, son?", Henri asks.

"Well, Mr Pélissier, seeing as how you've had enough, who do you think will win now?"

Desgrange fined Pélissier 600 francs for dropping out, for insulting Tour officials and for convincing his brother to leave the race as well. It's hard at such a distance to calculate just how much that represented in modern terms. A French government report, however, says that the average weekly wage in 1921 in Paris, where Pélissier lived, was 27.5 francs a day, so a fine of 600 francs was nearly twenty-two days' pay.[86]

Desgrange also ruled that any rider who dropped out and encouraged others to join him would be banned from the following year's race. He said that "any understanding among the racers in view of protests of any kind, or against the officials' decisions, any understanding to delay the finish etc, will be rigorously punished." This denied riders the rights that France had given employees since 1884 but it was never seriously challenged. Cycling needed Pélissier's union but nobody wanted Pélissier.

Albert Baker d'Isy (the creator of the Grand Prix des Nations, for years the world's unofficial time-trial championship) wrote of Pélissier in an obituary: "He had few friendships because of his absolute opinions, and the way he expressed them cost him many friends."

Years later, Francis Pélissier (Henri was murdered by his lover) smiled and said they'd been spinning Londres a bit of a yarn. The gist of the story was true, he said, but they knew he was a new kid on the race and they'd given him a better story because of his status. They had been exploiting his innocence to get back at Desgrange, who called Henri, accurately, a pig-headed champion.[87]

Left-wing papers made Pélissier a hero and denounced Desgrange as a capitalist exploiter of the worst sort. Right-wing papers like *L'Action Française* and *L'Intransigeant* accused Pélissier of destroying the very race that had brought him fortune and fame. In the end, the left's campaign was undermined from within. Almost comically, the union paper, *Le Peuple,* said that the most that could be deduced from the story was that Pélissier was, to say the least, irritable.

Even with its exaggerations, the story shows the condemning rules that Desgrange imposed. It was certainly true that he forbade riders to finish in fewer or indeed more clothes than they had started. The idea of putting lead in their pockets wasn't far-fetched: it was what was done in horse races, after all, to equalise the weights of jockeys. And at one moment Desgrange thought of insisting that all the riders eat the same amount of food. Only pointing out that large men need to eat more than smaller men, and that everyone had to eat copiously just to finish the day, made him relent.

The story of the water pump is accurate, too. Riders were forbidden for many years from carrying more than two bottles and team managers could not deliver refills. The outcome was not just the picturesque image of riders queuing at mountain springs or filling bottles from the hoses of obliging spectators but the less charming *chasse à la canette.* A canette is just that—a small can—and here it means a drink. But rather than take just soft drinks, and still less pay for them, team stars ordered their lesser riders to stop and rob bars.

Riders dropped their bikes at the entrance, ran inside, filled their pockets with bottles of anything they could find, then re-caught the race and distributed their booty. Photographers waited for it to happen and bar-owners, unable to lock the doors because they had customers inside, hid what they wanted to keep but let the riders plunder the rest.

Afterwards they sent their bill to Paris, doubtless with a little added to justify their trouble.

The British rider in the 1960s, Vin Denson, remembers Rik van Looy looking at him and commanding "Café!" Denson stopped at the next bar and got just that—a coffee. He raced back to the bunch and, pleased with himself, handed the bottle to van Looy. The Belgian sniffed it, swore and tipped the coffee on the road. It was then, Denson said, that he understood that *café* meant not just coffee but a bar. Van Looy wanted something stronger and from then on Denson obliged.

> VOICES FROM THE PAST
>
> Van Looy was a complete bastard. I never got the correct pay from Van Looy. He wouldn't tell you he couldn't pay you, either. He'd be all smiley but he'd get someone else to tell you.
>
> —Vin Denson

6
Bother with bikes

Drinks and clothes were nothing, though, compared to the trials that Desgrange put riders through with their bikes. It's not exaggerating to say that if Desgrange could have removed bicycles from a bicycle race then he would have. Long after aluminium rims became common, he banned them. He had raced on wooden rims and so, therefore, would his riders. Long after other races had allowed multiple gears, Desgrange still banned them. He wanted heroes, not Sunday-afternoon potterers. They were free to use freewheels but in the first Tour, in 1903, only Pierre Desvages is named as having one. Other riders thought freewheels risky. If they had to repair their bikes on the road, how would they mend one? That was a job to frustrate even experienced mechanics, but they at least knew the technique to stop the ball bearings and the spring-loaded pawls falling out. Exhausted and trembling riders trying to do it by moonlight stood no chance. Instead, they preferred to have a single cog on each side of the back wheel, stopping at just the right moment to turn the wheel and put the chain on a larger sprocket for going up hills. Later they fitted two sprockets on each side. But that was still direct gearing, meaning the pedals continued to turn when the bike moved and, equally, that the bike wouldn't move without turning the pedals. It was a treadmill which offered none of the modern respite of cruising down hills.

The Frenchman, Roger Lapébie, said: "We had big fork ends at the back of the bike to make adjustments possible. In the mountains we used a 44-tooth ring at the front with a 22 and a 24 rear sprocket on one side and 18 and 20 on the other. On the flat we had a 50-tooth ring at the front with 16-, 17-, 19- and 20-tooth sprockets at the back. You could lose a race if you didn't change gear at the right moment. There was a lot of psychology involved."

A lesser rider called Joany Panel sneaked a primitive derailleur into the Tour in 1912. Desgrange worried about others copying and banned them, and derailleurs were allowed only when Jacques Goddet took over in 1937. When Félicien Vervaecke anticipated the decision in 1936, Goddet docked him 10 minutes.[88]

Far more marked, though, was Desgrange's attitude to mechanical trouble.[89] Riders could be—and were—left to shiver uncontrollably in doorways, their fingers too frozen to unpick a punctured tyre, while an official stood by to be sure he asked for no help. That happened to Léon Scieur, from Floreffe, a town in Belgium best known now for the beer named after it. He punctured at least four times—some reports say six—on the way from Le Havre to Cherbourg in 1919. Having run out of spare tyres, he took a needle and thread from the handlebar pouch that he and many riders carried and, cold and soaked from a storm, began unpicking and repairing the tube.

Tubular racing tyres are known in America as sew-ups because the fabric casing, with its glued-on tread, is sewn around the inner tube that holds the air. For Scieur, the repair meant cutting the loops of waxed cotton to reveal the rubber tube, patching that and then threading a needle to sew the tyre back together again. It's a job which even now many riders prefer to pay others to do.

After a while, the woman who lived in the house beside which he was sheltering opened the door and offered to help. Scieur told her his fingers were too frozen and he was shivering too uncontrollably to thread the needle. Standing over him, a Swiss race referee, Lucien Cazalis, snapped: "It is forbidden to receive help. If Madame threads the needle, you will be penalised." Scieur eventually got the job done and set off once more towards Cherbourg. He lost the race to Firmin Lambot, another Belgian, by about the time he'd spent in the doorway.

In 1929, Victor Fontan of France was thirty-six and hadn't until then dreamed of a prominent cycling career because he had been shot in the leg twice during the war. To his surprise, and close to his home at the foot of the Pyrenees, he was wearing the yellow jersey of leader when he fell and snapped the forks of his bike. He walked through the early morning by the light of the moon, banging on doors to ask for a bike to borrow. He got one and pedalled on into the darkness but, making little progress, threw in the towel with the race leader's colours still on his shoulders.

> VOICES FROM THE PAST
>
> This Pyrenean had the blood of a true man of the mountains. Little, strong-backed, all muscle, what strikes you most with him is the contrast between the calm and tranquil expression in his look and the rough shape of his face.
>
> —Alex Virot on Victor Fontan, in *Match l'Intran*

> VOICES FROM THE PAST
>
> Today, my brothers, we meet, if you accept, in common and pious thought to address the divine bicycle. We will tell her of our piety and gratitude for the ineffable and precious joys she provides us: for the memories with which she has already filled our sporting memories and for what she has made possible today. For me, I love her for having made my soul capable of understanding; I love her for having taken my heart with her spokes and for having encircled part of my life in her harmonious frame.
>
> —Henri Desgrange, *L'Auto*, 1911

All this is nothing, though, compared to the well-told story of Eugène Christophe. The Hippo, as the other riders called him because he excelled in mud and rain, broke his front forks as he came down the Tourmalet in the Pyrenees in 1913. He was twenty-eight and the race favourite. He hadn't long come over the top of the mountain, in those days on an unmade road, when he felt his steering give way as he picked up speed. Some reports say it was after being hit by a car.

"I was on a straight stretch of road," he said, "and the bike started floating and it jammed. I slowed and then I saw it was my front wheel. I was devastated. I had lost the Tour de France there. I was something like eighteen minutes ahead in the overall standings and… I set off walking in my cycling shoes, with a leather bar under the soles [early versions of modern cleats] with the bike on my right shoulder and the front wheel in my left hand. The other riders were going past at sixty kilometres per hour. My legs were ruined by the time I got to the village. It was a true Calvary."

Not having a choice, he let the Belgian rider, Philippe Thys, continue the descent and he started to walk, sometimes with his bike on his shoulder, sometimes sobbing.[90]

"I was happy to have him off my wheel," Thys told *La Vie au Grand Air*, "but I was sorry for his having an accident that pushed him down the race."

Christophe reached Sainte-Marie-Campan at the foot of the descent after two hours and asked for the blacksmith. He had been racing since three that morning and the day's 326 kilometres had already taken the surviving riders over the Osquis, Aubisque, Gourette and Soulor climbs before the Tourmalet. The Aspin and Peyresourde remained to be tackled. Astonished locals pointed him down the road towards Bagnères-de-Bigorre. On the right, a little distance from the last house, he would find Henri Lecomte's forge.

Lecomte was at home when Christophe banged on the door and, watched by a small crowd, officials of rival teams, and a race manager called Mouchet, asked if he had the right tubing, then if he could use the forge and tools. He was no blacksmith but he been a lock-maker, so he had practical skill in his hands. "He was a nice man and he wanted to help me, but he wasn't allowed to," Christophe told *Sporting Cyclist* years later.[91] "The regulations were strict. I had to do all the repair work myself. I never spent a more wretched time in my life than those three cruel hours in M. Lecomte's forge."

Lecomte remembered that Christophe worked wearily but methodically, rarely speaking.

At one point Christophe had his forks in one hand and a hammer in the other. The fire had to be pumped to its greatest heat. That demanded a third hand that Christophe didn't have and according to one report he allowed a boy called Alexandre Corni to work the bellows for him. Or, according to the referee's report, to turn the drill to create the three holes that Christophe needed. Mouchet fined

Christophe a further ten minutes, later reduced to three in a moment of rash compassion.

It would have taken a lot less time had a spare fork blade been available but it wasn't and Christophe had to shape a piece of straight tube. Or so the story goes, anyway. Illustrations of the moment show that he is working not on the forks—in the picture they have been removed—but on the frame tubes where they join the steering column. This is uncertain history but it does seem more probable that it was the frame and not the forks that broke. Added to which, a frame could be repaired after a fashion by anyone prepared to take advice, whereas fashioning a new fork blade to a standard that the wheel would turn without rubbing is perhaps asking a little much. Nevertheless, Christophe insisted it was the forks and now and then he returned to the Tourmalet and the point at which they snapped.[92] And forks said to have been his now go on display now and then.

You would expect the story to be the sensation of the following day's *L'Auto*. But, no. All it gets is: "In a collision, Christophe broke the forks of his machine and had to walk as far as Sainte-Marie-de-Campan, a descent of fourteen kilometres. At the moment of telegraphing this story, he has lost more than two hours and I have no news of him."

There was no mention of the forge the day after that, either. The most that *L'Auto* could report was that "As for Christophe, so unfortunate the day before last, believe me when we say that he is planning a dreadful revenge [*il aspire à d'éclatantes revanches*]. His three and a half hours of delay have left him little chance of winning but he has lost none of his courage despite that." If there was to be a legend, it was to be neither immediate nor thanks to the reporting in *L'Auto*.

The astonishing thing is that Christophe finished his repair and set off racing again, riding back through Sainte-Marie-de-Campan and going straight up the col d'Aspin, which starts at the other end of the village. He reached Luchon at 8:44 p.m. in twenty-ninth place, and still faster than fifteen of the rest. Thys won the stage and went on to win the Tour.

Thys, by the way, signed his first pro contract for 300 Belgian francs a month. His father refused to believe that anybody would pay his son such an unbelievable sum—the price of the most expensive racing bike on the market—"for doing nothing." Thys produced the contract and his father read every word and then called in a lawyer, convinced that Peugeot was trying to trick his son in some way he couldn't work out.[93]

The forge is no longer there but a house stands on the spot, opposite the sign at the entrance to the village. The plaque commemorating the day spelled Christophe's name wrongly—as Cristophe—and that's how it remained until the Tour got round to replacing it on its 100th anniversary in 2003. Go back to the village centre and there on a plinth beside the church you can see an unconvincing sculpture of Christophe, three and a half metres high, holding his broken forks. Beneath it are the words, in French, "You never abandon a job you've started", followed by Christophe's signature.

That would be story enough were it not that it happened all over again in 1919. He was riding the 468 kilometres from Metz to Dunkirk—a slightly longer route than the one on which Léon Scieur broke his wheel—when the forks snapped once more. He had to mend his bike once more but this time he was luckier: there was a bike factory a little further up the road. The repair still took close on two hours, though, and he slipped from first place to third. Readers of *L'Auto* were so distressed at this new bout of bad luck that they sent him the money—and more—that he would have won without the accident. It took twenty lists in the paper to name all the contributors. They began with Henri de Rothschild with 500 francs and ran down to gifts of just three. Together, they sent 13,310 francs.

Christophe died at age eighty-five, in February 1970. He had never stopped cycling and right up until his death he crossed Paris for weekly meetings of his cycling club at Puteaux, usually with a cigarette in his mouth and a flat cap on his head. He is buried, with a yellow jersey, in the cemetery at Malakoff, the southern district of Paris now just outside the city's ring road, in which he spent most of his life. He was as close to Desgrange's cycling superman as any one man was likely to become, although he never won the Tour.

VOICES FROM THE PAST

In the 1911 Tour we were still using ordinary nuts on our hub spindles, and brakes which operated on the front tyre. Then next year came two very important improvements: cable brakes

> and wing nuts. Wheel removal was still difficult, however, with ordinary fork ends and chain adjusters. In the middle of the 1912 Tour, Christophe had an inspiration: there was rapid work in the Peugeot factory, and at Perpignan every bike in their stable was fitted with forward-opening drop-outs. For a time, it was almost a pleasure to puncture.
>
> —Firmin Lambot looks back fifty years

So why did they do it? Why did they do it, when for all that they were professionals, most got little more than what they could win and what they could negotiate for their presence? The better ones rode for bike factories—at that time only companies in the bicycle business had the right to sponsor riders—but even they received only minor wages and expenses in addition to their bike and jerseys. And most got not even that, some riding races at their own expense, including the early Tours, finding themselves hotels after a day's racing or, in one extreme case, performing gymnastic tricks in the street to raise the price of a bed.

The most colourful was a policeman from Nice called Jules Banino. Nothing pleased him more than a challenge. The writer Roger Dries said: "You saw him in all the sports events ever organised. There was a swimming meeting? He'd be the first to turn up, perched on his bike, and he'd dive into the sea and take part. A pole-climbing contest? Banino would be there. He once even took on the same wager as the Count of Monte Cristo, tying himself in a sack and being thrown into the Mediterranean at Tabau-Capeu. He almost drowned. He had to be pulled out in a hurry and he was hardly breathing when they got to him."

He was thirty-two when he rode the Tour in 1924. That summer was hot and so dry that he was blinded by dust and one day he finished outside the time limit. He was thrown out. That night, having no money for a hotel or a train, he set off to ride to Nice. So, a little later, did the race. The custom was to stay in a group until dawn, riding fast but with no attacks, because that was what the stars had ordered. That night, though, word reached the peloton that a lone rider was ahead of them, and going well. The stars looked around. Everybody who mattered was there. The escapee must therefore be a lesser-light. Well, he was going to be taught a lesson.

The peloton stepped up the pace. And finally, they spotted a lone rider. His style confirmed that he was indeed a racer and not some farm boy.

"Who are you?" the stars demanded. "I'm Jules Banino, an amateur. I'm just riding home at my own pace."

It wasn't a tactful way to put it: the greatest riders in the world had just been forced to spend an hour chasing him.

"We don't believe you!" someone shouted and the race leader, Ottavio Bottecchia, gave him a thump. The others joined in and one, the Frenchman Jean Alavoine, kicked Banino into a ditch. The problem now was that spectators had turned up from nowhere, even in the night. And not having seen the start of the row, they assumed it was Banino who was attacking and their hero who was defending. Delighted to join in, they began giving Banino a further good kicking, and then everyone went off and left him. He never rode the Tour de France again. He died at the age of fifty-four in 1947.

So why did they do it? The answer is that most were from poor rural families, to which cycling was, as boxing was elsewhere, a rare chance to progress. As the writer Christopher Thompson put it: "What is generally glossed over in the transformation of Tour riders into moral exemplars is that the event that conditions their public elevation is a professional competition, and their motivation is first and foremost economic. Tour racers have typically hailed from humble backgrounds, enjoyed limited career options, and faced a lifetime of modestly paid and often unpleasant labour should they fail at cycling."[94]

And the Tour liked that humble background, the fight to rise from mediocrity to stardom, says Jean-François Mignot in his paper on the economic history of the Tour: "The Tour organisers insisted on this aspect to encourage such dreams in its followers. For instance, as early as 1925, *L'Auto* published a series and participated in the making of a silent, multi-episode movie entitled *Le roi de la pédale*, featuring a working-class boy climbing the social ladder thanks to the Tour."[95]

Octave Lapize made his name in the Tour but, for him, it was a job. He was never keen on it. He was French national champion in 1913 when he stopped on the road to Brest, pulled in at a restaurant, ordered a meal and turned his back on the road. "The Tour isn't *une bonne affaire* [profitable] for me." he said. "I'm the only one in the team fighting to fill the coffers and some of my men are more demanding than they have a right to be. If I win the Tour, and that's not a given, it'll bring me at most 7,000 francs. Track contracts get me more than that. And, anyway, I've had enough. The moment I stop for a piss, the others attack and clear off as fast as they can go. But if an important opponent punctures, nobody moves. So I've had enough."[96] His point was made when most of the others in the La Française team then also gave up: only Lapize was making them money and there was no point in carrying on without him.

Desgrange's life depended on bike factories, their money, their owners and the riders they employed. He turned a deaf ear and may secretly have enjoyed being called Bostock for a while but, outside the office, he tolerated not the slightest opposition. He once fell out with a bike-maker called Émile Mercier, who had a factory at St-Etienne. Mercier died in 1973 and his company filed for bankruptcy in 1985, but his name lives on because of the team he sponsored for fifty years and, particularly, its star rider: Raymond Poulidor.

The row with Mercier began not with him and certainly not with Poulidor, who wasn't even born. It started when André Leducq, one of France's top riders, left the Alcyon team to join Émile Mercier. In revenge, Alcyon's boss, Edmond Gentil, pushed Desgrange into leaving Leducq out of the national team for the 1934 Tour. In those days, which we'll come to, Desgrange picked all the French teams himself. Mercier, of course, was cross. Leducq had cost him a lot of money and now he wouldn't get a ride in the Tour. So he complained. And did Desgrange care? No. Like all Desgrange's decisions, this one was correct, final and indisputable.

Mercier wrote complaints and then got lawyers to write still more. Desgrange retaliated by ordering his staff never to mention Mercier's name again. The problem was that Mercier was a team sponsor and a bike-maker and sometimes there was no option but to print his complaints. So *L'Auto* compromised by misspelling his name. People are touchy about their names, especially when they know they're being ridiculed, and back Mercier would go to his lawyers. *L'Auto* would then correct the story while taking care to get the name wrong once more.

"Monsieur Gercier has let us known that his name is Monsieur Mervier", it would write, and then a few editions later: "Monsieur Mervier asks us to say that, in reality, he is called Monsieur Cermier." When the aggrieved and non-existent Monsieur Cermier wrote once more, *L'Auto* excelled itself: "Monsieur Cermier insists that in fact he is known as Monsieur Merdier." *Merde*, put politely, is French for excrement. Peace returned only in 1954 when, Desgrange long dead, Jacques Goddet invited Mercier to follow the sixteenth stage of the 1954 Tour in his official car.

Who won the battle? Mercier on points. He contrived to make Leducq a correspondent of *L'Auto*'s rival, *Paris-Soir*. Leducq could then follow the race from which Desgrange had banished him and also write for Gaston Bénac, the editor, who drove Desgrange to a frenzy by printing each day's Tour results on the evening of the race. More than that, *Paris-Soir* looked snappier—"a paper has to be seen before it's read", Bénac believed—and it had a *bélinographe*, a wire machine with which it could instantaneously send pictures along telephone lines from distant parts of France and even abroad. It could not only report the stage winner to its growing number of readers—circulation rose to two million, making it the best-selling paper in France—but it could print a picture of him doing it.

Nothing was too much for him to get the news first. Bénac hired two small planes, five motorcyclists, five cars and a bus, bringing out an extra, late edition. *L'Auto* was forced to report its own race as old news next morning. And why wasn't it a knock-out for *Paris-Soir*? Because Desgrange swung a right hook by starting all the stages later in the day, to make the finish too late for Bénac to report.

In 1929 a fire swept through the Paramount studios in Hollywood. The actress Clara Bow, on hearing the news, is supposed to have said: "I hope to Christ it was the sound stages."[97] It happened that she was right: it was indeed the pioneering sound studio that burned. And why did she and other actors rejoice? Because not only did sound force them to act differently but it put a lot of actors out of work. Who wanted a cowboy with a German accent? How believable was the British actor Reginald Denny going to be now in his roles as an all-American boy? A great star of the period, Raymond Griffith, is now forgotten because a throat injury meant he could talk only in a loud whisper.

No cyclist was put out of work by the arrival of the Pathé newsreel at the 1930 Tour—"news with sound and speech"—but a lot of people were surprised that stars they had until then seen only in newspapers or flashing by on the road had thick Toulouse or Lille accents. Riders grimy and exhausted from the road were now sometimes asked to speak as well. For some, like Antonin Magne, their inability either turned away the cameras, to the dismay of their sponsors, or it made their name. Magne became known as The Taciturn and it became a novelty just to see him say anything at all. Little by little, a rider's contract came to depend not just on his legs but on how well he could speak in public, on the attention that he attracted. The Tour had become not just a race but show business.

Not that there was a lot of coverage. Look through the Pathé catalogue for the Tour that year in 1930 and you find just one entry, two minutes and six seconds, presumably one of a number of subjects that made up a newsreel. It had been only eight years since *L'Auto* had allowed other companies' journalists at all. It wanted the race to itself. It had founded it and it wanted exclusive coverage. But then someone in the office realised that it was missing publicity, that other papers could add to the romance of the Tour but only *L'Auto* had the pages to give it its full depth. So rival papers would be advertising *L'Auto*.

Ten other press cars arrived and Alex Virot made his first broadcasts for Radio Cité. He was a novice. What he hadn't foreseen was that the time it took to set up all the equipment to cover the Tour's start at Le Vesinet in a bow of the Seine west of Paris was wasted if he couldn't then report on anything else. The riders went off down the road and then there was nothing more to say. Broadcasts would have stayed a curious novelty were it not that Jean Antoine was there at six in the morning when Victor Fontan, the leader of the race, stood sobbing by the fountain at St-Gaudens. Desgrange's rule that riders could accept no help from other riders or their teams had forced him to go from door to door in the night in the hope of borrowing a bike.

Fontan sat sobbing at the foot of the fountain and Antoine was there with his elementary tape recorder. A little less than two hours later, the sound of his crying was broadcast in Radio Cité's news programme. Not until the following morning did newspapers have the story.[98] The power of audible sobbing led Louis Debblat of *L'Echo des Sports* to protest: "How can a man lose the Tour de France because of an accident to his bike?" Not only did that alert France to the power of radio but it forced Desgrange to relent. There were, after all, limits to what a superman could be asked.

Antoine learned fast: in 1932 he and Alex Virot, then with *L'Intransigeant*[99] but also working for the radio, recorded the sound of the bunch crossing the Aubisque, in the Pyrenees, on 12 July. They couldn't get a live signal from there, so they sent it by phone line. That was no mean achievement: recording anything on tape for radio had started only a year or two earlier. Next morning, *L'Intransigeant* devoted all its back page to the Tour, with a summary by Charles Pélissier but not, so far as I can see, any mention of Virot's contribution.[100]

Desgrange realised a page had turned. The historian, Jean-François Mignot, says radio made long, exhausting stages pointless. "Listeners were interested in direct reporting from the finish. Airtime being short, radio stations were prepared to broadcast something only if it attracted more listeners than the programme it displaced, so there was no point in having racing days as long as they used to be."[101] Where in 1926 the stages averaged more than 335 kilometres and lasted more than fourteen hours, the distance fell by 100 kilometres between 1927 and 1939. And the more stations could be encouraged to spend more time with the race, the more the Tour reduced the length and duration of stages and cut the number of rest days.[102] That was too late for Henri Pélissier, who had long argued with Desgrange about the length of stages, complaining that they weren't races but tests of endurance. The future was in more racing and fewer kilometres.

Radio took off and lifted the Tour de France with it. Surveys showed that outside broadcasts including the Tour were among the most popular of the 1920s.[103] And that changed the Tour, which now had to ensure that riders reached the line at the end of the afternoon, when the audience was greatest. More than that, though, it changed the style of reporting. In the Tour's epic era, when riders were alone with their fate on the road, that was exactly what they were: alone. There were no reporters with them. Writers had to collect stories afterwards from riders too exhausted to talk coherently and happy to make the most of their miseries. Corroboration wasn't possible. Newspapers need good stories to sell, and the sale of papers paid the reporter's wage. The temptation is obvious. If one paper printed a more dramatic account than another, readers would conclude they were buying the better paper. They weren't likely to compare papers and conclude that at least one of the writers must be making things up.

Desgrange gave nicknames to riders back in 1903 to make unknowns familiar. By the 1920s their names were known and the job of reporters was to turn them into heroes, the supermen which Desgrange had craved. That most riders were half-literate labourers who depended on their brawn more than their brain didn't matter. In print, everyone sounds the same. Radio took that away. It reported races as they happened and when they happened. A good commentator could make them more exciting but he couldn't make them up.

"The strength of sports reporting," Jacques Goddet wrote in his autobiography, *L'Equipée Belle*, "is to be unpredictable and intrinsically original. To tell the battle being fought beneath your eyes, at the very moment that it happens, what a privilege! You stick a microphone between the hands of just anybody and, provided he's voluble, that he has good diction, and we call them 'radio reporters', a sumptuous title, a race of journalists rich with the gift of the gab. But, then, the new way had to suffer the excess of incompetence of the over-zealous." Goddet, you will notice, not only preferred press reporting but took his writing style from Desgrange—only with fewer adjectives.

Immediate reporting killed the stories of lonely assaults on cold and bear-haunted mountains. But it brought immediacy, suspense. Listen to one report and you couldn't miss the next. It was so captivating that the British journalist Jock Wadley used to fasten a radio to his handlebars so he could listen to the race as he rode around France to write features for *The Bicycle*. In time, Wadley himself reported on the radio, for a sports enclave within the BBC's classical music station.

The next step was to film the Tour. The snatched images of Pathé newsreels grew to longer, more polished reports, some shot from beside the race as it moved. Crowds flocked to cinemas in an era before television made the Tour a day-long wallpaper of continuous reporting. Photogenic riders like André Leducq were solicited by film-makers and the stars exploited the studios in turn, turning their growingly familiar faces into advertising attractions, endorsing anything for a fee. Leducq's rich Marseille accent, still unfamiliar to most French people, contributed to his popularity—which showed in the description that "he was liked by women, whom he honoured as frequently as his track contracts." He spoke English like Inspector Clouseau, which didn't stop his trying to sing *On Ilkley Moor Baht 'at*[104] at five in the morning in a Parisian nightclub after a few drinks with the British cycle trader, Ron Kitching.[105]

7
The monster turns

By 1933, Desgrange had been driven to distraction. What had started as a simple campaign to jeer at smelly cyclists going home from the track without a shower had become a monster that repeatedly turned its claws on him. Whatever the formula he found, however cruelly he applied the rules—to be a judge or referee in Desgrange's time made you a mere servant to his wishes—his riders proved cleverer than he was.

If he made the stages long, they dawdled until the last hour. But if he made them shorter, he would be undermining his quest for the unbelievable. If he made them ride as individuals, they combined in groups, sharing the lead, deciding between themselves what speed they would ride at, with the single proviso that they didn't make it obvious when officials or photographers were about. As well as that, the roads were often too bad to ride close behind another rider safely, and that explains all those pictures of experienced riders taking care not to ride on each other's wheel. It also explains why there were barely any of the mass crashes that became more common later.

If Desgrange tried to get round the dawdling by awarding points according to finishing positions, the riders worked out there was no point in chasing a fugitive twenty minutes up the road if he couldn't catch him: the points would stay the same whether the gap was one minute or twenty. If Desgrange stopped the dawdling by going against his original rule forbidding team work, by making teams race in a giant team time-trial, the difference between the teams' strength killed the drama.

> VOICES FROM THE PAST
>
> The bugle sounds anew; Thys and Hector Heusghem sprint for a second place. Mottia pushes Vandall against the hurdles to the right, where both fall five yards from the line; Scieur, Masson and Lambot profit by the occasion to pass them. Barthélemy passes me with a front wheel, snapped clean in half, strapped on his back, a borrowed one in the forks… The men are loaded with three or four spares, food for four or five hours in a satchel, and a waterproof.
>
> —Vernon Blake, *Cycling*, 23 September 1920

He tried it, though. The 1928 Tour was a team time-trial on the flat stages. It was also the year that three Australians and a New Zealander planned to ride with six Europeans. The *Melbourne Herald* started a campaign and Dunlop, the tyre-maker, said it would pay their fare. The problem was that Hubert Opperman, Percy Osborne and Ernie Bainbridge of Australia and Harry Watson of New Zealand (who looked more like a priest than a professional cyclist) found no Europeans waiting to join them. Only four, and largely inexperienced, they were outclassed by teams that had ten riders each.

René de Latour[106] wrote of them: "Even if I live to be 150 years old, I shall never forget the sight of Opperman being caught day after day by various teams of ten super-athletes, swapping their pace beautifully. The Australians would start together. Bainbridge would do his best to hang on, but his passing years had taken more of his speed and he would generally go off the back after fifty miles or so. Then if it was not Osborne it was Watson who would have to quit at the hundred-miles mark. And almost daily, Oppy would be left alone for the last fifty miles." And there he was regularly swept up by and eventually adopted by the powerful Alcyon riders. The time-trial idea quietly vanished.

No matter what Desgrange did, he was thwarted by the imbalance of teams, the bloody-mindedness of riders or what he suspected were the machinations of the teams' sponsors. He had created a race, a new sport, but in his mind even those who gained most were determined to ruin it. More than that—and more cynically—trade teams now had riders from several countries. Their interest was that one of those riders should win; the rider's nationality was less important to them than his success. To Desgrange, it was the other way round.

If, say, a Belgian rider won a French race for Alcyon, then Alcyon was more inclined to buy a large newspaper advertisement in Belgium than in France. It bought a smaller advertisement in France because, frankly, French readers wanted to read about French successes and not those of Belgians. The smaller advertisement brought less money to *L'Auto* and so therefore did a Belgian victory, because it also sold fewer papers. The paper's circulation was falling.

And so, in 1930, Henri Desgrange came up with an idea that lasted three decades, a plan that changed the face of the Tour and which many a pale-eyed old fan in the bars of rural France still thinks was the *real* Tour de France: a race not for individuals, not for sponsors but between nations. From now on, riders would compete as they did in the Olympic Games, for the honour of their country. It was, as the British writer Geoffrey Nicholson pointed out, much easier to shout "*Allez la France!*" than "*Allez Mercier-BP!*"

L'Auto waited until the world championships and the end-of-season races were out of the way and advertised the new Tour over the central three columns of its front page on 25 September 1929, signed by Desgrange himself. Such a change, a modern mind would say, demanded an exciting headline. Instead, *L'Auto* chose the unrevealing "The 24th Cycling Tour de France" and didn't hint at the changes even in the small headline that followed: "*Sa formule—Son itinéraire—Ses étapes—Son règlement.*" Readers would have to read.

The sponsors protested, of course, until it dawned on them that they could still advertise their riders' successes, albeit in another jersey, but now have the Tour pick up all the costs. Desgrange was now committed to providing their hotels, their food, their travel costs, masseurs and mechanics, and even their bikes—a bonus at a time when sales were starting to fall.[107]

Providing bikes wasn't wholly necessary but Desgrange was out to stop the sponsors getting even a gram of advertising that they hadn't paid for. He ordered yellow bikes for every rider and marked them only with the name of his paper. Alcyon was happy when journalists found out that it had the contract to build them because it was forbidden to boast of it. Alcyon got the job, speculation said, because the one team manager to raise a proper objection to national teams was Ludovic Feuillet… the influential manager of Alcyon. Desgrange was happy to keep him quiet and to see that Alcyon's involvement was leaked to the papers.

On top of that, Desgrange said he'd be happy to take success advertisements from the everyday sponsors even though their riders were on different bikes. Feuillet couldn't reasonably say that one of his riders had won *on* an Alcyon, because the contract said he couldn't, but he *could* say that a rider under contract to Alcyon had won. That solved the advertising problem and the costs of the race could be raised by charging for publicity vans to precede the riders and by demanding that towns pay to welcome the race in return for the trade and publicity that it brought.

The Tour had never been as pure as the ascetic Desgrange had hoped but now it had properly sullied itself. And the involvement of outsiders' advertising in his race helped in time bring about *extra-sportif* sponsors, investors from outside the sport.[108] They put money into the sport that bike companies could no longer afford but they were also less interested in advertising in a purely sports newspaper. There is rarely a victory without a defeat.

VOICES FROM THE PAST

The caravan of sixty vividly painted trucks that sing the virtues of an aperitif, or of underwear or rubbish bins makes a shameful sight; it shouts, it plays bad music, it's ugly, it's sad, it's horrible—it's the vulgarity of money. That M. Desgrange accepts parasites on the course, that's fair enough; but at least he could impose a minimum level of decency. A rolling circus, no!… The day that M. Desgrange, who is very intelligent, understands that, he will sort the matter out with two strokes of his pen; and I never give up hope of one day seeing among the staff of the Tour de France, a commissaire of good taste.

—Pierre Bost, *Marianne*, 10 July 1935

Dirty Feet

Riders were told to turn up with their own saddle and handlebars and reported to *L'Auto*'s office forty-eight hours before the race to collect their bikes. As one of two Britons in the three-man Empire team of 1937—we'll return to that in a moment—Charlie Holland remembered: "At once we were supplied with a machine each, spare tyres, goggles, waterproof riding jacket and a suit case to hold our spare clothing during the Tour. The idea of the latter is that everyone shall have similar equipment, thus discouraging riders from carrying more than necessary. Some of the riders left to their own choice in the matter would send large trunks on the lorries that take our baggage ahead from stage to stage.

"It is usual for the rider in the Tour de France to fit his own saddle and handlebars, and we spent the best part of that day fitting these items to our machines, adjusting the gears, brakes, etc. All the bicycles are painted yellow, with black lines (*L'Auto* is printed in black on yellow paper), and on the head tube the name of this newspaper is transferred, whilst on the top tube is painted the name of the rider. No advertising of any description is allowed in connection with the bicycles we ride."[109]

There are still some of these yellow bikes around. I rode one once, it was battered but complete. It had a single gear, steel cranks, and wing nuts to fasten the wheels. The frame angles were relaxed and the front forks had a generous rake, both of them to cope with the bad roads. Another one, in an exhibition at Marmande in southwest France, had two sprockets on each side of the wheel. Four gears, therefore, but no way to change from one to the other without hopping off and undoing those wing nuts, sometimes called butterfly nuts (cautious riders used to carry a spare, in case they dropped one in the grass during the night). The slots for the rear wheel pointed forward, more usual for a derailleur, and not backwards as is more usual for a fixed wheel—that innovation from the Peugeot factory. The brakes were steel, side-pull and primitive, the levers unpadded.

Now, you don't come up with plans to entirely change the Tour de France in just a few weeks. It's impossible to imagine that Desgrange and the others finished the 1929 race, went back to Paris to handle the paperwork, and then off on holiday and yet had everything arranged by 24 September, ready for the following day's paper. Desgrange had been brooding over his race for years, planning, plotting and calculating in his château beside the Mediterranean. He'd been brooding since way back in 1911, when a heavy-browed and occasionally moustachioed French rider, Maurice "Coco" Brocco, realised he could never win the Tour himself and began instead to sell his help to whoever would pay. This, of course, he didn't advertise outside the peloton. To anyone who knew the sport, though, it was clear. Brocco had done a deal with the François Faber—the hero of the First World War whom we encountered a while back—to pace him to the finish.

Desgrange didn't dare disqualify Brocco on the spot because he didn't have the proof and because he worried that Brocco would protest to the UVF, the national body. The UVF was in awe of Desgrange and often did what he wanted but that weak-kneed compliance couldn't be guaranteed. Instead Desgrange lambasted Brocco in *L'Auto* and said he was unworthy of being in the race if the best he could do was act as a *domestique*—a house-cleaner or, by implication, petty servant. A battle of wills ensued, Brocco sneering at Desgrange and taunting him but finally shooting himself in the foot by his arrogance. When Brocco proved he was a lot more than a petty servant by breaking away alone in the mountains to win a stage by thirty-four minutes, Desgrange took that as proof that he had been slacking earlier and disqualified him.[110]

Brocco's name has now all but vanished from the sport—he lived until 1965 and the age of 82—but the word *domestique* has stayed as a word for a team man, a rider employed to close gaps, carry water bottles and generally sacrifice his chances for his leader. The word no longer implies an insult.

What drove Desgrange to irrecoverable anger, though, was the Tour of 1929. There, everything he disliked and feared became obvious. "My race has been won by a corpse" he half-lamented, half-sneered. The use of the word "my" shows the relationship he had with the world's greatest race and its riders.

So what had happened? Well, Maurice Dewaele, a Belgian from Lovendegem, north-west of Ghent, had taken the yellow jersey in the Pyrenees after the leader, Fontan, broke his chain. That already gave Dewaele a tint of unworthiness but worse was to follow. When the race reached the Alps, Dewaele suffered so badly on the Galibier that next morning he was still unconscious when the race was due to restart.

At one point he'd been unable to eat solid food and got by on sugar dissolved in water.[111]

Desgrange delayed the race for an hour so that a soigneur—a cross between a boxing second and a quack doctor—could bring him round. Which he did but not totally. His colleagues in the Alcyon team then flocked around him and pushed him and threatened any rider inclined to take advantage. They had that power because such was Alcyon's dominance and mystique that journalists used to spend the day hanging about at its workshops in the knowledge that they'd get a story and that just Alcyon's name would give it headlines. As de Latour wrote in *Sporting Cyclist*: "Famous men used to collect their bikes bright and shining on a Friday and Saturday and take them back on Monday covered with dust and mud. The Alcyon *service des courses* was a happy hunting ground for cycling journalists."

Anyway, Dewaele won the Tour when under any other circumstances he would have been sick in bed, and Desgrange never got over his hurt pride.

If it wasn't riders themselves ruining his race and his quest for a superman—that had vanished when the Tour was won by "a corpse"—then it was their sponsors, especially (but unnamed because it was an advertiser and too powerful an adversary) Alcyon. "For twenty years I've been searching for the ideal formula and this year we couldn't find it," Desgrange accepted.[112] And so came the decision to keep the riders but get rid of the sponsors. From now on, teams would ride for their country. And Desgrange would pick the countries and choose the French teams himself with the aim of keeping out trouble-makers in general and Dewaele in particular.

National teams would rid him of the aggravation of trade sponsors. That was plenty good enough. What he didn't realise was that that would also bring the Tour its most romantic decades, when those beside the road could recognise the blue jerseys and then shout for France.

National teams brought French the self-confidence that had vanished in the Franco-Prussian war and had then become doom-ridden by the devastating losses of the First World War. But more than that, they brought a boost for *L'Auto*'s sales, which had stagnated after reaching 500,000 in 1924 and now continued to fall. There hadn't been a French win since Henri Pélissier in 1923 and France was losing interest, at least in buying papers to read about foreigners.

The logistical problem was that there weren't enough cycling countries in Europe to put up a full field. Some countries didn't even have enough riders for a team. Holland, for instance, a country we now see as a giant of the sport, didn't even allow races on the road in 1930.[113] All it had was track racing and the officials it sent to the Tour in its first years for national teams had never raced with brakes and freewheel. The riders had; the men dictating how they rode never had.

Desgrange got round the shortage by allowing smaller countries to put up combined teams—the entire British Empire managed three riders, you'll remember—and by taking in the less talented, the latter-day equivalent of the buccaneering *touristes-routiers*. He grouped them into regional teams, sometimes associated with regional newspapers, to make up the numbers and to spread *L'Auto*'s sales by introducing local favourites. When that wasn't enough, he was open to offers from any group of riders who'd offer themselves as an identifiable group.

That, for instance, was how Romania came to have its sole team in the Tour even though the Romanian cycling federation says now that it knows nothing about it. In 1936, Gheorghe Hapciuc, Virgil Marmocea, Nicolae Tapu and Constantin Tudose lined up for the start on 7 July. Old photos show them in matching pale jerseys with a dark chest band. Not one of them made it beyond the third stage.

Bucharest had told me it knew nothing of this first team. When I e-mailed back with the names, back came the reply: "These riders were not professionals." And yet they must have been, and they must have had professional licences from a national cycling body somewhere to be able to ride. So who or what were they? Well, it took some searching but they were four of Romania's best, despite the national association's ignorance, and it turned out to have been the national association that nominated them. But it had no money and so the four travelled to France at their own expense, with neither a manager nor a mechanic. They finished the first stage together an hour after the winner after 258 kilometres. Tudose fell on the second stage and finished outside the time limit. The other three took two minutes more than they were allowed after 161 kilometres from Charleville to Metz and they were sent home. Desgrange was keen on sending riders home early in the race because it saved him hotel and food bills.

This ad hoc eagerness to make the Tour international was how the British Empire had that three-man team. Only Holland got beyond the first week and Pierre Gachon, a Canadian, went home on the opening day after being left behind on the first hill.

Holland had entered as an individual a month earlier. Two weeks before the start, the editor of *Cycling* gave him a copy of *L'Auto* which said that he would not after all be taking part. *Cycling* sent a telegram to Paris. *L'Auto* replied next day via *Cycling*'s office in Birmingham, where Holland lived. It said: "Following your wire dated yesterday agree engagement if you agree yours—*L'Auto*." And that was how Holland found that he would be representing 412 million people and a quarter of the world's population.[114]

Only France, Belgium, Italy, Spain and Germany had the full eight riders that morning of 2 July 1930 when the former winner, Antonin Magne, flagged them away for a long preliminary ride around Paris.[115] Desgrange, with a freedom of word that later generations find discomfiting, categorised each—"the Spaniards, small and blackish, very reserved and without airs; the Germans, the living opposite of the Spaniards, tall and blond and more imposing; the Belgians with their familiar faces and calm through their experience of the biggest races; the Italians, petulant, bubbling, talking fit to burst; the French, those you know already, so there's no need here to describe our own race."[116]

Along with the national teams were pick-up squads for the North, Normandy, Midi (the south), Provence, Côte d'Azur, South-east, Alsace-Lorraine, Champagne and the Île-de-France (greater Paris).

VOICES FROM THE PAST

Giants of the road… grandiose sports event etc. Those are just a couple of the clarion calls that the Tour de France inspires—this year like those before it—in the *petite-bourgeoisie* whether they're sporty or not. Communists refuse to prostitute the word "sport" and its hard and disinterested joy by associating it with the commercial calculations of so-called sportsmen. Bottecchia, the little Italian builder, appears to have won the 150,000 *livres* that he

> estimated he needed for the happiness of his family. But for every Bottecchia who rises from proletarian misery to the deceptive comfort of the *petite-bourgeoise,* how many other riders remain labourers of the road for ever?
>
> —*L'Humanité,* a communist daily, 21 July 1924

If France were to win then it would be best if French riders could help each other. As the Dutch historian, Benjo Maso, wrote: "The riders of the French *équipe nationale* didn't owe their popularity just to their wins. The national-team formula brought a whole new aspect to the way they rode. Desgrange had written in the rules that a certain level of team spirit would now be allowed, provided it wasn't abused."[117] Where once Brocco and Dewaele had been seen as regrettable but inevitable commercial contrivances, now those alliances were called friendship and patriotism.

French papers called their 1930 riders the Friendship Team. The riders went along with it, of course, posing with arms around each other's shoulders, a picture of perfect harmony. But that was the public face, which itself had its own commercial benefits because a bit of *entente cordiale* would do wonders for their fees in village races after the Tour and then on the track in the winter.

The reality was different. There was no reason that former rivals should get on more, or overcome years of aggravation, just because Desgrange had put them in blue jerseys with white and red stripes. Look now at snaps of Charles Pélissier entwined with André Leducq and you'd take them for pals. The reality is that they disliked each other and that they formed a regular pairing on the track only because they won more together than they would apart. It didn't make their life better that Pélissier was paid 3,500 and even 4,000 francs to ride on the track and in village races while Leducq, for all his protesting to organisers, often got less than 2,500.[118]

On the other hand, Pélissier was Beau Brummel and his charm and elegance sold tickets. And if there was any doubt of his worth, he dispelled it in 1930 by winning eight stages and finishing second in seven others. Sprinters, however, win by fractions of a second; winning the whole race takes a lot more. Leducq won by more than fourteen minutes but still his contract fees stayed below Pélissier's. In the end contrasts and frictions like that ruined the ambiance in the French team and their run of wins ended.

National teams were a hit with crowds. They could identify them by their standard colours, the French in blue, white and red, the Belgians in pale blue with red and yellow bands, the Dutch in orange. Even now, experienced eyes look back nostalgically. The eyes, for instance, of Bernard Morlino in *L'Équipe Magazine* in 2003: "To see the Italians, the French or the Belgians competing between them in the colours of their country produced an excitement that's absent in the battle of trade names. In football, France versus Brazil sounds better than Adidas versus Nike." Raphaël Géminiani, who rode in that era and then managed teams in the commercial years, recalled in his autobiography that "riders in national and regional teams fought for a jersey, which made sense; they rode themselves to death for our colours and the public knew it, they approved and they shouted encouragement."

Among those who would like national teams to be reconsidered is David Lappartient, then the president of the French federation and later head of the UCI. The often-cited problem that teams would be influenced by their commercial alliances, their riders unwilling to cooperate with national team-mates because the rest of the year they were paid to be rivals, is one that goes back to 1930, which influenced the Tour then and until the 1960s but didn't spoil it for spectators more interested in a spectacle they could understand.

Lappartient said: "In football, there's the European club championship but there are also the championships of Europe and the World Cup for national teams. One doesn't hinder the other—far from it! And then, for a national federation, it would also be a way to impose stricter ethical rules. I know that teams say 'If my sponsor doesn't get into the Tour, he'll pull out.' That may be true in France but, for me, the fact of putting national teams back in the Tour, I'm convinced, would make other races more attractive if we had a redrawn and corrected calendar. Having a football World Cup doesn't mean fewer people follow the champions' league. We need that duality in the calendar. So many people can't see further than what they know."[119]

The new national colours soon produced a popular hero, a man to sacrifice his chances for his leader and his country. No matter that the legend is better than the truth. The man concerned was a lightly built climber called René Vietto. The legend began even before he started cycling. It said he had been a humble lift-operator in Cannes, on the Riviera. René de Latour is more specific and says it was in the Palais Croisette.[120] Such a humble job showed he had submitted his life to others right from the start. The story was accepted for decades—until some awkward journalist went through the employment records of all Cannes' hotels that had lifts and found he hadn't worked for any of them.

No matter, the legend is that he was going up and down in his lift when he met the Italian giant, Alfredo Binda, who suggested they go training together. His advice is said to have paved the way for Vietto's ride in the Tour of 1934. The most famous picture of Vietto, as he sits on a roadside wall, seemingly alone and in tears, comes from that Tour.

The leader of the French team was Antonin Magne, who had won it three years earlier and who later had a long career as a team manager, notably of Raymond Poulidor. Among Magne's eccentricities was a belief in diagnosis by magnetism—he regularly held a magnetised needle over Poulidor's body to see which way it circled—and that he forbade his riders from wearing jerseys with zipped necks. You have only to look at pictures of Poulidor when he rode for Mercier to see that that was so. As though that weren't enough, Magne while a team manager dressed in a cowman's white smock, addressed all his riders as *vous* rather than the more casual *tu*, and was notoriously difficult to interview because he was so tongue-tied.

Magne's racing career ended with the German invasion of France in 1940, during which he lost all his yellow jerseys in the confusion. In 1934 he led from the second stage in a race in which France won nineteen of the twenty-three stages. It did wonders for French morale and enthusiasm and Vietto's sacrifice just made it more sympathetic.

Magne was the star and Vietto a twenty-year-old novice in the Tour whom many said should never have been selected. The two were leading the race as they came down the col de l'Hospitalet in the Pyrenees on the way to Ax-les-Thermes. Magne wrecked his front wheel in a crash and Vietto stopped to give him his—one of the sacrifices for which he's always remembered.[121] *One* of the sacrifices because almost the same thing happened the next day, this time to Magne's back wheel, on the Portet d'Aspet.

This time Vietto was a little ahead. Magne shouted for him to stop. Vietto didn't hear but a German rider, Ludwig Geyer, passed the message. Vietto looked over his shoulder, turned in the road and rode back to where Magne stood with one wheel already out of his bike. There were no neutral mechanics travelling in cars or on motorbikes in those days so once again Vietto had to wait for the line of slow-moving trucks with their team spares to reach him.

Vietto had surrendered his hopes to his leader, who won the Tour to such acclaim that he was invited to ride alone along the Champs Élysées. He had won by more than twenty-seven minutes. The crowd was said to be greater even than that which had welcomed the Armistice in 1918. France had triumphed, had found its superman and his suffering acolyte, all in national colours. So much for the legend. The truth is that Vietto and Magne had little time for each other. Years later, Vietto said: "I didn't give him the wheel. He took it. It was a hold-up and I should have complained."

Some have tried to calculate that Vietto would have won the Tour had it not been for the two successive sacrifices. He came fifth. But Magne won, remember, by pushing on for half an hour. Vietto was just eight seconds short of an hour behind him. The delays on the mountain had cost him ten minutes at most. And Vietto lost the Tour not on the climbs but on the flat and on cobbles, because his lightness denied him the strength to match the fastest. He even took to living for a while in northern France to master the cobbled roads there and in neighbouring Belgium. He lost time particularly in races against the clock, yet when he started training on the flat and riding bigger gears, he succeeded only in becoming heavier and less talented as a climber.

The other point to this story, which again shows the way that France invested itself in the hopes and tragedies of its heroes, is that the classic picture of Vietto shows him alone, sitting on a stone wall with one leg drawn up and one foot on the ground. His bike, carrying the number thirty-eight, lies with its back wheel on the verge and the empty front forks on the wall. The picture's message is that he was alone in tears on the mountain, sacrificed and abandoned by the older man, looking down the hill with tears in his eyes as he waited long minutes for help to arrive. France had a superman and a super-martyr.

See the full negative, though, and you see he was far from alone. He has a small crowd of the sympathetic and curious to one side of him. They were cropped out before the newspaper was printed. France needed what Desgrange saw it needed: supermen alone in their battles, and journalists whose living depended on keeping that faith were happy to go along with it.

Vietto was talented but he was difficult and often depressed, unsmiling, socially awkward and eccentric, insisting among other things on mounting his brakes on the unconventional side of their fixing. He had a dozen frames made for him once and one by one rejected them all. He argued over jerseys. Once, in a television interview, he was reminded of a Tour time-trial in which his hopes had vanished.

"It was like seeing a man commit suicide," the interviewer suggested.

"Monsieur," Vietto answered solemnly, "I have had suicidal tendencies since I was seven years old."

He made a fortune in appearance fees in village races that autumn of 1934 and earned more than a victory in the Tour would have brought. But he was neither the first nor last cyclist to entrust his money to a smooth-talker with big promises and smaller talents. The man was named Trailoux and Vietto's money vanished. Vietto retired to run a pig farm in the hills, near his boyhood home at Rocheville. He became cranky and resented visitors. He died in October 1988, a broken man and still a committed communist.

Supermen are for films, not real life. And it all came to an end. French riders fought among themselves as their sponsorship salaries fell. The money they won became more important than ever. Not only could a good ride in the Tour double their salary but it would bring in still more in appearance races on the road and track. In 1938, Magne and André Leducq crossed the finish line of their last Tour with their arms round each other's shoulder. The crowds went wild. It was the last flap of the butterfly's wings. Next year Europe went to war.

Dirty Feet

VOICES FROM THE PAST

André Leducq is the greatest road rider in the world this year, because he has won the Tour de France against the best riders, the biggest test in the world. He is a pure child of France. He has the clear face of our race. He is quick-witted and intelligent… He blossoms with health. He looks you straight in the face and all his being cries that life is good in France.

—Henri Desgrange, *L'Auto*, 27 July 1930

8
Love and politics

Desgrange remains a legend. His initials appear on the yellow jersey that he invented and which has been copied across the world ever since. They disappeared for a year or two, then returned. There is a street named after him in the Bercy area of Paris. It runs north-east from the suburb's giant arena. You pass one end of it when you take a train in or out of the Gare de Lyon. He married but quickly divorced, although not before the couple had a daughter, Denise, and—it's not clear—perhaps at some stage an adopted son, also called Henri. Little is known of either of them, except that both kept their distance afterwards. As did his brother, the archive clerk.

In fact, it's hard to work out Desgrange's attitude to women, not so much whether he liked them as whether he found them entirely necessary. He didn't just stop at his advice that a racing cyclist had no more need of girls than of yesterday's socks: he wrote that a cyclist who befriends a woman puts a block on his handlebars and a cobblestone in his pockets. He simply banned wives, all women, from the Tour. The ban continued into the 1970s.

That produced a smile from Charles Pélissier, whose very name for years produced sighs of happy memory from lovers across Europe. The rule, he said, "confers a serious advantage to the unmarried and the irregulars of all categories"[122]—although Jules Merviel, who crashed on the way to Marseille in 1935, fell in love with his hospital nurse and married her. I do like the tactful reference to "irregulars of all categories."

The one woman Henri really loved was an avant-garde artist called Jane Deley. Or perhaps she was the one person in the world who could dominate him, which he would have both resented and respected. It's easy to see him as fascinated, entranced, uncertain, like a teenager

Desgrange's big secret: work." A deep photo showed him running in shorts and with impressive thighs in the mud of a cross-country. There were two more columns on the front page next morning as well, with the headline "The father of the Tour" and an appreciation by the race's general secretary, Lucien Cazalis (the man who stood over Léon Scieur to make sure he accepted no help as, shivering, he tried to thread a needle to repair a tyre). It ran on to the back page, the paper by then reduced to a single sheet printed on both sides. Next morning again, there was a further tribute—"He lives on"—written by Jacques Goddet. There was more again on the twentieth, the twenty-first, and the twenty-second. By the twenty-third the coverage and tributes had moved from the front to the back. And, there, there was still more on the twenty-fourth, the twenty-fifth, the twenty-sixth, the twenty-seventh, twenty-eighth, twenty-ninth and thirtieth. Only then did the paper stop.

Or, rather, it didn't. The first day of September brought news that the Friends of Henri Desgrange planned to put up a monument and, on the back page, seven paragraphs were headed "Farewells to Henri Desgrange", with more next day. Nothing on the third but he was back on the fourth, fifth, seventh and ninth. Then on the tenth it started all over again with the whole back page, framed in black, given over to many of the stories that had been printed in the month following his death. Desgrange did not pass unnoticed.

It's hard to work out now what happened after his death but there seems to have been a row between Deley and Desgrange's former wife, who until then had expressed no public interest in her former husband's affairs. Deley wanted to bury him at their home at Beauvallon while members of his family seem to have wanted him interred in Angers, where his daughter Denise lived, or in a family grave at the Père Lachaise cemetery in eastern Paris. Search the internet and there are references to Desgrange's being at Père Lachaise. Search the names of those confirmed as buried there, though, and he's not there. Chopin is there, Oscar Wilde is there and so is the singer Edith Piaf.[123] But not Desgrange.

His burial has turned into an Agatha Christie mystery. There are persistent stories that his body was transferred to the family grave at Commentry, in the department or county of Allier, at the insistence of his former wife. Whether she and Desgrange had formally divorced is also unclear.[124] The argument goes on but the probability is that he is still buried at Beauvallon, where his grave is a low two-tier structure of black and grey marble with his name in gold capitals. He lies next to Jeanne Deley, as she is styled, who died in July 1949 when she was seventy.

Oddly, neither *L'Auto*, its successor *L'Équipe*, nor the Tour de France itself thought to build a monument, put up even a modest plaque, to the man who had brought them all about. Nor did the mysterious Friends of Henri Desgrange. The monument that stands now at the col de Galibier was paid for by public subscription. That there was nothing in Paris came as a surprise to the Italian, Gino Bartali, after he won the Tour in 1948. He did his lap of honour at the Parc des Princes and then picked up the two bouquets he had kept rather than throw them to the crowd. He took them with friends to the Pied de Cochon restaurant in the rue Coquillière, near Les Halles, then Paris' great meat market. The restaurant had opened the previous year and it's still there. Bartali was ostentatiously religious and a friend of the Pope, who had sheltered him during the war and helped him avoid fighting in the army.[125] One of his bouquets was to go to the Notre Dame cathedral in Paris, to lie at the statue of the Virgin Mary. The other was to go on Desgrange's grave. That, he discovered, was closer to Italy than to Paris. He gave it instead to Jacques Goddet and asked him to place it where he thought best. It was then that Goddet realised there was nowhere to put it. So he ordered a plaque for *L'Équipe*'s offices, and Bartali laid the bouquet there, stood silently for a minute and then left for a paid village race in Belgium. When he unpacked his suitcase there, he found someone had stolen his yellow jersey. In those days riders got only one.

L'Auto had become *L'Équipe*. *L'Auto* appeared for the last time on 17 August 1944, a paper that looked as sad as its time and circumstances. Two columns beneath its title explained: "*L'Auto*, since 25 July 1940, was forced to appear, and it did appear, first by being printed at the *Lyon Républicain* at Lyon, then from Paris, in the Occupied Zone, finally in publishing from July 1943 an edition in Lyon for which the entire content was transmitted from our offices in Paris by telephone or telegraph. The partial interruption of phone communications, telegraph and the railways has forced us to suspend *L'Auto*'s appearance until further notice in the southern zone."[126] That was discreet waffle. The truth was that on that day, 17 August 1944, *L'Auto* was forcibly closed because it had printed German propaganda and news.

The Second World War, like the first, began barely after that year's Tour had concluded. Tensions were rising and German, Italian and Spanish teams stayed away in 1939. The race ended on 30 July and the war began on 3 September. For France, it ended nine months later, with the armistice of 22 June. By then, *L'Auto* belonged to Germans. In the 1920s, Victor Goddet had persuaded Jules-Albert de Dion, one of the founders of the paper and the man who was there when the president was roughed up at Auteil, to give him all his interests in *L'Auto* or to sell them to him at a giveaway price.

De Dion obliged and Goddet thereby shared his interests in the paper, in the Parc des Princes and in the Vélodrome d'Hiver indoor track close to the Eiffel Tower with his brother, Maurice. Where Victor was steady and careful, Maurice was a party animal. He spent, spent, spent and when nothing was left by 1938, he sold his shares. He sold them to a press baron called Raymond Patenôtre, who lived in a mansion he had designed himself in the rue de la Faisanderie, two streets back from the Bois de Boulogne in Paris.

Patenôtre had been born in 1900 in America, where his father was French ambassador. His mother was an heiress from Philadelphia. In one of those curious turns of the period, Patenôtre moved from supporting an organisation protecting Jewish rights in central Europe to printing a newspaper in France that was sufficiently pro-German that he came close to being tried and executed for collaboration. He escaped the shooting squad because he fled back to America at the start of the war. He directed his papers from there and gave his orders to his business manager, Albert Lejeune. It was Lejeune—who founded Paris–Nice—who got shot, but not before selling Patenôtre's shares in *L'Auto* to the Propaganda Abteilung run by the Germans. The paper therefore came under the control of the Occupant.

The start of the war had put *L'Auto* into financial problems because sports meetings stopped and there was little to report. Desgrange filled what would have been blank spaces by printing a news-in-brief column called *Savoir Vite*. Before long the Germans took it over and filled it with Occupation news as a condition for *L'Auto*'s continued appearance. Just how much that upset Desgrange and Jacques Goddet has never been clear. They may not have liked the Occupation—few people did—but they were realists and businessmen. They supported, or never objected to, the increasingly pro-German government of Philippe Pétain which nominally ran all France but in practice only the southern zone.[127] That makes neither a collaborator but nor does it make them *Résistants*. France, desperate for any leadership after the debacle of invasion in 1940, had greeted Pétain the old first-war hero enthusiastically and almost unanimously; it was only afterwards, and fairly quickly, that disillusion set in.

Émile Besson, who reported on thirty-five Tours for the communist daily, *L'Humanité*, concluded: "The two points are that, first, Jacques Goddet in what he wrote was a long-time supporter of Marshal Pétain. The second is that *L'Auto* scrupulously published all the Nazi propaganda communiqués."[128] When, in 1942, 7,000 Jews in Paris were rounded up and for the most part imprisoned in the Vélodrome d'Hiver, it was Goddet who gave the keys to the Germans. He may not have had a choice. But there was what the police call "previous." Goddet had allowed the French Nazi, Jacques Doriot, to hold his pre-war rallies at the velodrome. Perhaps it was just business—but the way in which neither event gets more than a token mention in Goddet's autobiography raises eyebrows. He gives extensive coverage to events of no interest at all, including his childhood bike rides and his theory that Israel should be moved to Australia, but barely anything about a moment so terrible that French presidents for years refused to acknowledge that France was to blame.[129]

On the other hand, Pierre Chany, who worked beside Goddet for years after the war, said: "Jacques Goddet, during the war, looked after the business, kept the shop running. In a way, yes, he was passive concerning the Occupant, but that was no more than ninety-eight per cent of the population in 1940."[130] The researcher Frédéric Pierre says that the 1,200 articles that Goddet wrote under the heading of "From one day to another" showed persistent support for Pétain.[131] When Pétain took over the administration of France by abandoning the republic and introducing an ethic of family, work and patriotism instead of *liberté, égalite, fraternité*, the national motto since Napoleon, Goddet wrote: "In 1940, France is starting another life. The Marshal [Pétain] will give it a bath of purification."[132]

At the end, he became a *résistant de la dernière heure*, a patriot happy to fight for his country when it looked certain the Germans would lose. When the inquiry came, as it did, he pointed to how he had joined the assault on a ministry building occupied by the Germans. He could say that his printers, under Roger Roux, were printing Resistance leaflets and de Gaulle's speeches in his building. He said that supporting Pétain was to support the national government but not collaboration. He also said that the paper would have printed far more pro-German articles had he not been there to stop them. But they were lame excuses: he had become a *résistant* only when there was no danger to himself and when the end was near. And, as for printing Resistance leaflets, it appears that he had no idea what was going on.

The inquiry was held in Algiers, which in those days was still part of France. It wasn't convinced. It decided that Goddet and *L'Auto* had supported Pétain and comforted the Germans. Things were so bad that Goddet came close to being jailed or shot or left to be maltreated in the mob *épurations*—purifications—that saw those perceived to have cooperated, especially women, beaten and publicly humiliated. The judges didn't go that far. But nor did they let him keep his paper. The doors were locked, the possessions sequestrated and the paper closed.

It is hard and unfair to judge the past with what we know in hindsight, with the standards we have now and with the knowledge of how the story ended. Some in France sided or at least accepted the presence of the Germans because they saw it as the least bad option. If the British were about to be invaded and conquered, and if the Germans were unbeatable and if, as it seemed then, France really was to be part of a Thousand-Year Reich, then best to get along with them and bring the war to an end. Whoever won, it wasn't going to be France. Ordinary people had to keep the sewers working, the water running and the trains in operation. It was what they did. Things would be worse if they didn't, so they went to work as usual. A few were outright collaborators and profiteers and by and large they paid the price. As did Pétain's prime minister, Pierre Laval.[133]

Dirty Feet

Goddet prided himself that he hadn't run the Tour de France under the Occupation, although it is difficult to see how he could have even if he wanted to. The Germans would have provided what he needed, as far as it was available, because their policy was to make Occupation seem as normal as possible. But where would the riders come from? What condition would they be in? How would the race cross from north to south and back without opening the doors to escapees, in the race and outside it? What would have been the reaction of the population, struggling on tiny rations, to a hundred fat-cat cyclists enjoying themselves in a parody of national celebration?

Both Albert Lejeune and his successor at Paris–Nice, Jean Leulliot, came out of the war deeply stained. Leulliot moved from *L'Auto* to the ultra-collaborationist (despite its name) *La France Socialiste*. There he did what Goddet did not, which was to promote an ersatz Tour with the agreement of the Germans. He called it the Tour of Europe, according to the historian Michel Dalloni, to make it easier to sell to the Germans.[134] It appealed to their idea of a pan-European Greater Germany.

The Circuit de France, as it was then more modestly renamed, started on 28 September 1942, and by 4 October it had passed through Le Mans, Poitiers, Limoges, Clermont-Ferrand, St-Étienne, Lyon and Dijon before finishing in Paris, where it had started. Pierre Laval was at St-Étienne to meet the riders and congratulate the organisers. The riders included some of the leading names, all from occupied countries no longer at war: from France, Émile Idée, Guy Lapébie, the climber Benoît Faure, Pierre Brambilla and, from Belgium, Stan Ockers, Marcel Kint and Briek Schotte.

Laval was shot as a collaborator in the closed courtyard of Fresnes prison in Paris soon after noon on 15 October 1945, hours after trying to commit suicide. Leulliot was lucky not to have come to the same end. Soon after the war he made friends at *The Bicycle* in England, where presumably his wartime activities weren't known. He was a friend later with editors of *Cycling*. Jean Bobet, however, uncovered a less friendly story when he wrote his history of cycling in wartime France.[135] He says Leulliot threatened to report Émile Idée to the Gestapo if he didn't ride. "I asked him to say it again to be sure that I had understood", Bobet said. "Victor Cosson [third in the 1938 Tour, who was also present] looked at him aghast. He hadn't known."

Leulliot was tried but saved by the support of fellow journalists. It's impossible to say now how that happened. It may have been simple solidarity between professionals, although the same didn't happen for many other writers. More likely is that they didn't know—riders didn't complain, Bobet said, for fear that they would be sent to Germany in the national forced labour scheme,[136] and journalists could just have thought he was stupid, naive but that his heart was in the right place. He was organising races, after all, and without races they would have no work.

As it happened, the race was a catastrophe. The distances were much longer than advertised and the race ran late day after day. Riders lost their way in the mountains of the Auvergne and had to be rescued. Louis Caput was away by himself without an escort or a following car when a man waved his handkerchief in the half-light of dusk to get him to stop. It was the only way he had to tell Caput the race was ending there and not going its full distance.

Goddet wrote in his autobiography: "Do you understand, Jean, up there above us, why I have never since shown any bitterness towards you? This shameless demonstration was enough to stop the attempt ever being repeated. This 'great first' Circuit de France has remained… the only one." It's hard to know if Goddet was choosing his words diplomatically long after the event. Why? For two reasons. The first is that in 1954, the Tour de France started in Amsterdam, its first foreign start. Curiously, that was also the year that Leulliot held his first Tour of Europe. The bigger event—Goddet's—stole the interest of the smaller, just as he intended. And then later, while the company behind the Tour de France was only too happy to buy failing races all over Europe, it showed no interest in helping Leulliot when his Paris–Nice struggled. Leulliot's widow sold it instead to Laurent Fignon, in 1999, for 4.5 million francs.[137] The Tour de France company, ASO, bought it from him two years later.[138]

The outcome of all this is that *L'Auto*'s office was boarded shut, a fate it shared with 187 other papers deemed to have bent to the German will. The paper, Goddet wrote in his memoirs, had "fallen into the communal grave of public dishonour." Everything that *L'Auto* owned passed to the Société Nationale des Enterprises de Presse, a government body that would have to decide how to redistribute them. Paper was in short supply and the priority was to start new general newspapers. Sports and other specialist publications had to wait until the armistice was signed in May 1945 and then the easing of paper rationing in February 1946.

With *L'Auto* gone and the Tour therefore in public hands until it could be awarded to someone else, there was competition for the right to a paper and especially to the Tour. Communists had been the driving force of the Resistance once the Germans had attacked the Soviet Union and, in peace, many of their ideas for social restructuring had been accepted by the otherwise right-wing Charles de Gaulle. The communists generally and the Resistance in particular had hoped, even assumed, that their leaders would form the post-war government. Communists were a considerable force in post-war France, with forty per cent of the vote, and they achieved a lot in their strongholds in the north and in industrial areas elsewhere. These, of course, were the days before Nikita Khrushchev's denunciation of Stalin disillusioned all but the most ardent of sympathisers. De Gaulle, who had known Stalin, had no intention of allowing a communist revolution in the country he considered his soul.

The communists, you'll remember, had an influential daily paper called *L'Humanité*. It still exists and it is still strong on social and political injustice, although these days it is the last struggling whimper of the committed rather than a roar. It still sends two reporters to the Tour every summer, reporting with a good eye on the race but never unaware that they are in the hall of the enemy. One of the reporters, Jean-Émmanuel Ducoin, says that France's post-war winner, Jacques Anquetil, always voted for Roland Leroy, a communist politician and one of the paper's directors.[139]

Over the years, *L'Humanité* has made much of the Tour's commercial exploitation of the misery of workers. While it conceded that riders had chosen to ride and were therefore in a different class from miners and other labourers, it pointed to the fatal crash of the Spanish rider, Francisco Cepeda, in 1935 and called him "one of those who make the fortune of the great profiteers of capitalist sport."

After the war, the communists also had an interest in two magazines, *Sports* and *Miroir Sprint*. Together, they applied to run the Tour. Legend says that de Gaulle himself stopped them and leaned accordingly on Pierre-Henri Teitgen, his minister of information. De Gaulle wasn't going to let a national treasure fall into the hands of not just political rivals but a party he saw as dangerous for France. Those on the right often saw France's widespread support for the communists as a door being pushed open to dominance by the Soviet Union. Their fears were fanned by the American CIA, which said it had an "authoritative" report of a Cominform conference in Poland that "the Soviet Politburo is directing a co-ordinated all-out Communist campaign to take over the French and Italian governments."[140]

That left just Goddet, the man who had only just been deprived of his paper because it and perhaps he had collaborated. Compromise is needed in politics. Goddet could at least point out that he had joined an infantry regiment, even if so little happened there that he and Jacques May, another journalist, had time to send back reports back to *L'Auto*, which from 16 September 1939 appropriately became *L'Auto-Soldat*.

Goddet's new paper, *L'Équipe*, could take over provided it recruited from the Resistance, provided it didn't use yellow paper, provided it didn't allude to its predecessor, and provided that Goddet was neither named in the list of journalists nor allowed to sign articles. His path towards editorship was smoothed by Émilien Amaury, the head of the Havas news agency and an impeccable figure because of his early association with the Resistance through a group called the Rue de Lille.[141] That association with *L'Équipe* and the Tour was to go further than Goddet could have guessed.

Goddet founded a company called Sopusi, for *Société des Publications Sportives et Industrielles*, and moved into four rooms at number 13, across the road from where he had been at *L'Auto*. They'd been discovered by Géo Lefèvre, the man who had thought up the Tour de France in that very road half a century earlier. Goddet and the conference table were in one room, the journalists in another, the accounts staff and others in a third, and the typists in a fourth. Lefèvre, whose job now was to find advertisers—"Géo, you're an ace!" Goddet used to say each time he found one—had a few square metres in a former lavatory.

Their first paper appeared on 28 February 1946. By then the staff had been allowed to move back across the road to number 10. On the first front page, Goddet wrote: "We are living through a cruel time in the life of a society in which, if we fail to resist it, selfishness will become the dominant passion. Against such a threat, we will fight in the name of solidarity. *Équipe* [team]—the very word exercises a noble influence on the heart of our group—an influence that was exerting itself during a time of rage and hope when our collective will was placed in the service of the Resistance." As agreed, his name did not appear. The reference to collective will being placed in the service of the Resistance was hypocrisy. Goddet no longer sought a superman but, once again, France's leading sports newspaper saw its role as more than providing football results: it was to fight against selfishness and to bring a noble influence. French writers do rather overdo the flowery to English-speakers' eyes but, purple prose or not, there was once more a mission to improve the people.

In time, Amaury came to own both *L'Équipe* and the Tour de France. In 1944 he started a paper called *Le Parisien Libéré*, which he ran as a workers' cooperative. Like *L'Équipe*, it had risen from the ashes of an earlier paper, *Petit Parisien. Le Parisien Libéré* still exists, its name reduced to *Le Parisien* in 1986, though it no longer belongs to the Amaury family.

Amaury and Goddet became equal shareholders in a company called the Société du Stade-Vélodrome du Parc des Princes and they bid to run the Tour de France. *Sports* and *Ce Soir* (an evening paper with a circulation of 478,000 and therefore pretty influential) also wanted it and, as a demonstration, it ran a five-stage race for trade teams, the Ronde de France, from Bordeaux in the west to Grenoble in the east. Twelve days later, *L'Équipe* held its Petit Tour de France from Monaco to Paris, from south to north, for national and regional teams. It was won by Apo Lazaridès of France at an average of twenty-nine kilometres per hour.

Neither company was allowed a race of more than five days because of rationing and food shortages. Having watched both races, it was for the government to decide which could go further. It chose the Goddet-Amaury bid, with Goddet as director-general and Félix Lévitan and Charles Joly as his deputies. Lévitan was a weasel-faced shopkeeper's son from the thirteenth *arrondissement* or borough of Paris who had started as a deliverer of newspapers for *Parisien Libéré* after the First World War, and risen to head of sports reporting there. Joly was a promoter at the Parc des Princes. The Tour de France was to ride again from 1947, following the borders of France except for the legs out of and back into Paris. The Ronde de France was won by Giulio Bresci, an Italian rider of lasting anonymity, and was never held again.

> VOICES FROM THE PAST
>
> This year's Tour de France was over only five daily stages, from Monaco on the Mediterranean, over the Alps, to Paris, instead of the usual month-long race, with its twenty-four daily stages. But the "*petit Tour*" was just as tough as the pre-war Tour. So tough, in fact, that if it had lasted a few days longer there would have been no riders left in the race, or at least very few. What made "the little Tour" so hard was the fact that the riders had to tackle the mountain stages of the Alps only one day after the start.
>
> —*The Bicycle*, 7 August 1946

The truth was that France in 1947 was in little position to do anything at all. Rationing was getting worse rather than better. The daily bread allowance was cut from 300 to 250 grams. The prime minister, Paul Ramadier, was cynically referred to as Paul Ramadan. Inflation ran at sixty per cent. A combination of communists and anarchists brought about a strike of 30,000 workers at the Renault factory at Boulogne-Billancourt. A month later, communists were excluded from the government. Strikes spread across the country. A police riot squad was formed. Governments fell one after another. And amid all this, Benjo Maso surmises, the government may have decided that anything that united the nation, however briefly, should be encouraged, that therefore the Tour should go ahead.[142]

It would hint at the return to normality, as the Germans had hoped a few years earlier—even if it needed nearly 20,000 litres of petrol, 1,000 kilos of meat, 950 chickens, 150 dozen eggs, 770 kilos of sugar, 160 kilos of cheese, 350 kilos of plums, 8,000 bananas, 18,000 oranges or peaches, 12,000 loaves, 16,000 cakes, 300 kilos of rice, 30 kilos of jam and 3,000 litres of wine.[143] That didn't go unnoticed by people queuing outside shops in the hope that there would be something to buy and then to eat. Dockers threatened not to unload ships bringing in Goddet's supplies, resenting the preference that cyclists were getting, but abandoned the idea when it became impossible to tell what was going where.

For Pierre Chany, "the restarting of the Tour after an interruption of seven years provoked an immense enthusiasm. A world now returned to peace was passionate for more peaceful jousts. The Tour was received as a party wherever it went. The advertising caravan was flamboyant and, every night after the racing, the nightlife in stage towns continued into the small hours, as if young people were trying to make up for lost time."[144]

Appropriately, the old era closed with the lauded sacrifice of René Vietto and the new opened with a hobgoblin of an anti-hero who bucked tradition and, so many believe even today, won a Tour he didn't deserve. Jean Robic, of course, always said that nobody rides a race but to win, which is what he had done. His own self-estimation, never subdued, was that he would have won no fewer than five Tours had he not been foiled by bad luck. Nobody but Robic seems of that opinion but what is undeniable is that his treachery on the last day of the race in 1947 led the man who *would* have won it to go home and bury his bike in the garden in frustration.[145] Or so, at least, legend insists. And—this is truth rather than fiction—Robic ended his days refereeing professional wrestling matches in which, thanks to his smallness, he was regularly thrown out of the ring. He was 1 metre 61 tall (5 feet 4 inches) and weighed just 60 kilograms (132 pounds). That's both shorter and lighter than most present-day women in France.

André Mahé, who won Paris–Roubaix in 1949 and was therefore a contemporary, told me that Robic ended his life a bitter man, looking for work or at least someone to whom he could repeat his stories. "When he went into a bar or a restaurant," Mahé said, "he would stand in the doorway, wait until he'd been noticed, and then shout '*Oui, c'est moi... Robic!*'"

Go now to the town hall at Radenac, a place of barely 800 souls between Locminé and Josselin, in the Morbihan region, and you may find there's still a room in the town hall dedicated to the village's son. The last I heard, the walls were still covered by photos of this curiously small and ugly man, with newspaper cuttings and explanations. For all that Radenac celebrates a son, he was actually born in the Ardennes, at Condé-les-Vouziers, in the bar in which his mother served beer. The Robic family was looking for work and the Ardennes were where carpenters were needed after 1918 and so that's where his father found a job. And where he rode bike races. In 1925 the family returned to the north-west, first to Rennes and then in 1927 to Radenac. Jean worked at making wheels for carts, rode races and in February 1940 moved to Paris to work as a bike shop mechanic. Three years later he turned professional, that same year meeting a girl called Raymonde Cornic, who worked in a nearby bar, the appropriately named Rendezvous des Bretons. The Tour historian, Jean-Paul Ollivier, described her as the most beautiful girl in Montparnasse.[146]

Legend says that Robic told Raymonde that he had no money but that he'd give her the Tour de France as a wedding present. And so just before the end of the Tour in 1947, he was close behind the race leader, Pierre Brambilla, when the race reached Rouen on the last day. It was tradition then as it is now that the race leader is allowed a final day of peace, to revel in his victory, to be seen by the fans. Yet leave Rouen towards the south-east on a road with a succession of numbers and you'll have a tough few moments as it rises to reach the suburb of Bonsecours. Keep your eyes open and you'll see a row of steps leading to an engraved, grey stone with a picture of Robic on his bike and, beside it, the explanation that it was here that he broke clear of the field on the last day, took the yellow jersey and won the first Tour de France after the war.

The last line explains: "The town of Bonsecours greets (*s'associe à*) this exploit." And it greets it—it's the only thing of note that has happened there—even though Robic was a foul-mouthed, barely literate man admired by those who favoured the uppity little man upsetting the system but seen by history as one of those unavoidable embarrassments that happen in even the best regulated families.

That day in 1947, the hill appeared on the closing stage from Caen to Paris. Robic was French and in the white jersey of France-Ouest, one of the regional teams. Pierre Brambilla, the race leader, was more complicated: Italian by nationality, born in Switzerland, living in France but not yet French by naturalisation. Italy hadn't been forgiven for declaring war against France and then occupying part of the Riviera.

Rather than invite a formal Italian team, the Tour had therefore recruited Italians living in France. This was intended to help but it just aggravated riders and fans even more, because Italians living in France had been suspected of being the Enemy Within. And that included Brambilla, who got the message and took French nationality two years later. In his own way, he was as colourful as Robic, swearing and even punching himself when he went badly in the mountains.

The race reached Bonsecours and Robic jumped ahead, believing he was about to win a prize for being first to the top of the hill. Brambilla was dropped as a result and Robic was joined at the front by Edouard Fachleitner, a member of the French national team. Fachleitner—who phoned home every night to talk to his dog—stood little chance of taking enough time to win the Tour, particularly if Robic was with him, so he proposed a deal. For 50,000 francs, he said, he would cooperate to keep Robic ahead of the field. Robic would then win the Tour and Fachleitner could come second. Robic agreed. And he agreed again when Fachleitner changed his mind and said he wanted twice as much.

The figures weren't hard to do. Fachleitner was asking only four days' worth of appearance money in the after-Tour village races. Robic's fee there as the Tour winner would rise far above that, and he'd be guaranteed a place in every race that could afford him, and he could ask far more for the following year's team contract.

Robic won the Tour by 3 minutes 58 seconds. He didn't win the stage, which went to Briek Schotte of Belgium, who'd been ahead all the time without Robic's knowledge. Fachleitner came second, as he hoped, and money changed hands. Brambilla, the man whom tradition demanded should be allowed his day of glory, came in third at more than ten minutes. Years later, he and Robic were friends again, drinking heavily together in the Gonfalon bar to celebrate an old-timers' race at Germigny-l'Evêque, north of Meaux, on 5 October 1980. The evening had been organised by Joop Zoetemelk, the Dutch winner of the Tour de France who ran a hotel in Meaux. Zoetemelk was related to the Gonfalon's owners.

The story is a little confused, perhaps because of the drink involved, but the gist seems to be this…

Robic came with a girlfriend. His wife had left him after the failure of their restaurant in the avenue du Maine in Montparnasse, after which Robic took still more heavily to the bottle and worked in a succession of humiliating jobs, including, as we've seen, being thrown out of the ring in wrestling bouts. He moved to ever smaller apartments, finally to one at 68 rue Didot, Montparnasse, above what are now a Chinese take-away, a key-cutting shop and a Thai restaurant. Drinking steadily until after midnight at the reunion, he hazily realised his girlfriend was no longer there. He went upstairs to room number six and found her in bed with another man.

He was furiously angry and staggered downstairs drunk, to storm out. Wiser heads—René Vietto among them—tried to persuade him to stay, to sleep off his anger and the drink. Robic refused. He went out into the night with a woman called Lianor Sanier, the wife of Robert Sanier, another former rider. He would be passing her house and could drop her off. Why she accepted to get in a car with a driver so drunk that the bar's owner had tried to confiscate his keys, nobody knows. It was a little after 3 a.m. At 3:30, twenty-seven kilometres later and on the Route Nationale 3 near Claye-Souilly, that with passenger Lianor he drove his Audi 100 into the trailer of a loaded truck from Luxembourg. The police thought he had fallen asleep, because there were no skid marks. Blood tests showed a more likely cause.

It's hard to know what Henri Desgrange would have made of Robic. Perhaps he would have celebrated his audacity, his willingness to race to the end. Perhaps not. Either way, the Tour changed with Desgrange's death, with the war and then with Robic. A man with dirty feet had won the Tour.

Hardly anyone who was a teenager in that period, let alone an adult, is left alive. We are looking at a world so recent but one we picture in black and white, when women wore heavy shoes and vivid lipstick and men wore raincoats and hats and competed to look as dull as possible. France had been invaded by both sides. It had been bombed by both sides. It had been pillaged by the Germans and wrung bloodless in demands that it pay exorbitant prices for the right to be occupied. There were more than a million prisoners in German prisoner-of-war camps, most of them captured when they faced impossible odds after the British took to the boats at Dunkirk. Close on half a million buildings were wrecked, five times as many damaged. Two children in three had rickets, visible in their bowed legs, after years of poor and insufficient food.[147] One in five boys and thirty-six per cent of girls were noticeably less tall than they should have been.[148]

Two streets from the palatial American embassy in the avenue Gabriel, opposite the Champs-Elysée gardens in Paris, is a blue plaque mounted on a wall. Thousands pass each day without a glance. It marks the signing of the Marshall Plan in the building on which it stands. The aid agreed upon in that building accorded a quarter of the funds to Britain and a fifth to France. In return, Europe agreed to buy American goods. It's also how America resisted the growth of communism in Europe, by tying its economy to those of the old continent.[149]

Recovery was fast. France spent as much or more on colonial wars as it received from America but enough went into restoration of society and production that the following three decades of spectacular growth that followed Marshall Aid are referred to still as *Les Trente Glorieuses*. The new optimism, the rebuilding of alliances, the first steps of commercial union with Germany that led to the European Union, all that made the Tours of the post-war decades the race's golden period. That was the case in France above all, where Louison Bobet, Jacques Anquetil and Raymond Poulidor may now be remembered in their careers only by the grey-haired but Poulidor—the last survivor—was such a symbol of good but difficult times that he was greeted warmly wherever he went until he died in 2019.

No wonder, then, that three weeks of cycling carnival, with the giants of the road by day and the giants of popular entertainment in stage towns at night, would create a wave of relief, escape and diversion in the lazy hot days of summer. In the middle of all this, a small boy in Concarneau, in Brittany, followed his first Tours on the radio. Jean-Paul Ollivier is semi-retired now but for decades he was the warm voice of French television commentaries, sometimes from a motorbike, more lately providing historical context not only to the race but the abbeys and castles over which the television helicopter circled as the race progressed.

"The best years were the Fifties," he told me in the office he held at *France Télévisions* in the fashion district of Paris. "Cycle-racing wasn't only at its peak but it was rich with personalities. After the war, Europe was looking for its own personality. Cycling provided that. That's what the sponsors and the teams have all but killed off. The riders, the teams, are [now] all the same. In the Fifties and to an extent in the Sixties, it was a *phénomène*. The riders could say 'I'm going to do it this way, my way'. And then, because Europe was moving again, there was a rivalry between nations—a good rivalry: France, Spain, Italy, they all had their champions. Cycling carried those nations' dreams. Now, it's as if they come off a production line."

Henri Desgrange would have loved all that. It was his introduction of national teams, after all, that had encouraged it. But otherwise he would have been out of place. He was a man of other times, of earlier wars, wars lost with Germany. He grew up when Frenchmen were more sickly in peace than they had been in war. He grew up when children left school young and barely educated—if they went to school much at all. Cycling in the 1950s was still an escape from life in the fields, mines or factories, but by the 1960s cyclists were progressively better educated than he had been.

9
Heroes found

Just as France needed heroes more worthy than Robic it got them: first, Louison Bobet and then, together, Raymond Poulidor and Jacques Anquetil. We have come across Poulidor already, the slow-talking peasant's son from a farm near Limoges, all dark hair and slow smile and wrinkled face, the opposite of Anquetil, who was a fair-skinned, high-cheeked Norman with an odd upper lip and intense eyes. Poulidor personified the France of tradition, of dependable values such as hard work and Catholicism. Money was something you earned and which you used to buy a cow—for which he was teased as an amateur—and not to be thrown about. The German rider, Rudi Altig, used to tell of the day that Poulidor drove him to Limoges for a race that they would both ride next morning. On the way, Poulidor pointed out where he lived—and then drove Altig on to his hotel rather than go to the expense of providing fresh sheets and giving him breakfast next morning.

Anquetil was everything that Poulidor wasn't—bony-faced to Poulidor's gentler lines, worldly-wise where Poulidor was happiest on his farm. Going off for his national service in 1955 was the first time Poulidor had even been on a train. By then Anquetil, who was two years younger, had been to Helsinki and won an Olympic bronze medal in the team time-trial and had, while still a teenager and not yet a full professional, won the Grand Prix des Nations. In those days it was the world's unofficial time-trial championship.

Anquetil was always portrayed as a city slicker, an atheist and the incarnation of a country that had risen from the heavy grasp of the Catholic priest and the depression of the war. In fact he was as much a country boy as Poulidor. He was born on 8 January 1934 at Mont-St-Aignan, which is part of the ancient city of Rouen, and his parents lived in the neighbouring suburb of Bois-Guillaume. His father, Ernest, was a master builder, and his mother, Marie, ran the house. It was in 1940, when Anquetil was six, that the family left the city to live eight kilometres to the north-east at Quincampoix. A dead straight road, the D928, connects the two.

Specifically, they moved to the hamlet of Le Bourguet, a kilometre and half away. "Paradoxically," Anquetil recalled, "I owe the freedom of my childhood in the countryside to the German occupation. In 1941 my father refused to take on the only jobs he was offered, which were German defence work. Just about overnight he threw in a job that he loved. My uncles grew strawberries and so that's what we were going to do as well. Better to accept the challenge than to compromise ourselves."[150]

Anquetil went to the village school with its teacher in clogs, a smoking stove and a smell of damp wood. He came top of his class but with as little effort as he could manage, a trait he displayed throughout his racing career. "I calculated my efforts according to the competition," he remembered. "Just like when I was on my bike, I knew when to make the difference when I had to. Why get fifteen or sixteen out of twenty when ten would be enough to be best in class?" His best subject: arithmetic.

Anquetil worked on the family smallholding when he was a boy but then went to the Marcel-Sembat *lycée* in Sotteville, a suburb of Rouen. The name is embarrassing because it means Drunk Town. There he studied metalwork and ran in cross-country races until a fellow student, Maurice Dieulois, told him in January 1947 that cycling was a great way to meet girls. That appealed to Anquetil, who would always be shy, and he joined the AC Sotteville, which was largely run by André Boucher, a cycle-shop owner and once the sort of professional who couldn't make a living.[151] Boucher saw his talent and, when Anquetil was eighteen, he entered him for his first race, the Grand Prix de Gai-Sport at Le Havre on 8 April 1951. Anquetil went home unplaced because the judges missed him when he crossed the line. His next race was the Prix Maurice Latour on 3 May 1951. He won. Dieulois said: "I saw a champion but not one of the level he got to."[152]

Anquetil left college to work in a local factory and then, twenty-six days later, he left there to be a bike rider after an argument about time off for training. The next year he won the Grand Prix des Nations for the first time. And here we come to an odd twist. Anquetil's fame in France spread beyond the country, this pale and still fleshy-faced youngster who had come from nowhere to beat the world's best riders against the clock. Dick Yates, one of the many who have written biographies of Anquetil, remarked on his subject's odd behaviour.

"Look," he said, "when Anquetil won the Grand Prix des Nations, he was an unknown outside France. He went [to Italy] to see Fausto Coppi, who was the big star. In all the pictures you see of Anquetil in normal life, he's very smartly dressed, a man who likes and can afford clothes. But when he goes to see Coppi, he puts on peasant farmers' clothes to give Coppi the impression that he's just a country hick and that Coppi's got nothing to worry about. And he plays the peasant again for his press pictures after the Nations. This is a man who's never been a farmer, who went to a city college. And yet the pictures he arranged or at least contrived in after the Nations show him feeding corn to chickens and wearing clogs. Not on his farm but his father's farm. Anquetil? In clogs?"[153]

It didn't take long before Anquetil could buy as many shoes—or clogs—as he liked. He bought a château with a pool and roamed the grounds at night to peer at the stars through a telescope. Poulidor left the family farm and had a house built at St-Léonard-de-Noblat, a town with a beautiful, ancient centre.

Anquetil won the Tour de France five times, the first man to do so. Poulidor never did and yet he was persistently more popular. Like the Rolling Stones and the Beatles, it wasn't socially permissible to like both. You had to choose. Pierre Chany told a tale about those days which, while no doubt fanciful and exaggerated or more likely just invented, gives a clue to the feelings that the two produced. "The Tour de France," he wrote, "has the major fault of dividing the country, right down to the smallest hamlet, even families, into two rival camps. I know a man who grabbed his wife and held her on the grill of a heated stove, seated with her skirt held up, for favouring Jacques Anquetil when he preferred Raymond Poulidor. The following year the woman became a *Poulidoriste*. But it was too late. The husband had switched his allegiance to Gimondi. The last I heard, they were digging their heels in and the neighbours were complaining."

Two sociologists put the divide like this: "Those who recognised themselves in Jacques Anquetil liked his priority of style and elegance in the way he rode. Behind this fluidity and the appearance of ease was the image of France winning and those who took risks identified with him. Humble people saw themselves in Raymond Poulidor, whose face—lined with effort—represented the life they led on land they worked without rest or respite. His declarations, full of good sense, delighted the crowds: a race, even a difficult one, lasts less time than a day bringing in the harvest. A big part of the public therefore finished by identifying with the one who symbolised bad luck and the eternal position of runner-up, an image that was far from true for Poulidor, whose record was particularly rich."[154]

There is a scene in the film, *The Commitments*, in which the camera pans slowly down a wall, showing first a photo of Elvis and then, below it, the Pope. Certainly in rural areas of France such as the Creuse, to the east of Limoges, such devotion to Poulidor wouldn't have seemed odd. They especially would have seen the sense of a teenager buying a cow. Fellow riders used to laugh that he had the legs of a stallion but the brains of his cows. And thereafter, whatever he did, he was outwitted by the calculating Anquetil, a man who never made an effort he didn't need to make—remember his test results at school—and never once crossed a col ahead of the field if there was no advantage to it.

Time after time Poulidor finished second to him in the Tour, a result that did three things: it won him the sympathy of all who felt sorry for the underdog; it made him a living through personal appearances and commercial contracts for the rest of his life; and it introduced an expression into French: to be the Poulidor of anything from a sports event to a political shenanigan is to not win. The historian Jacques Marseille, for instance, once wrote of France long after Poulidor had stopped racing that it was "suffering from a Poulidor Complex"—a lack of belief in itself.[155]

Anquetil was from Normandy and sometimes spoke with the local habit of sounding cryptic but making sense. When a reporter asked if Poulidor could ever win the Tour, he replied: "He'll only win if I am riding—and then he'll come second." It takes some analysing but what it meant was that only Anquetil's presence could bring out the best in Poulidor but that, since Anquetil would also be in the race, it wouldn't be enough.

Dirty Feet

There was no possibility, of course, that the two could share an agent. Apart from any clash of personal interest—which may not have troubled the agents themselves—there was a long period in which Anquetil and Poulidor wouldn't even talk to each other. They communicated through their wives, although the extent of that coldness has, both men have said, been exaggerated for popular effect. In those days, riders were paid or at any rate given bikes and jerseys by their teams and they kept what they won in races. The biggest rewards were from the round-the-houses races that followed the Tour. They were a considerable income even for stars and essential for lesser lights, who could ask a handful more francs in appearance money by virtue of having finished the Tour. Monotonous it may have been, riding round one village after another, but they were paid for starting and they kept whatever they won. By contrast, they got nothing for starting the Tour and five daily hours of racing could bring them nothing at all. No rider could contact all the promoters and nor could the promoters sign all the riders. Instead, each side went through agents. It avoided the situation that Louison Bobet had found himself in, when he was billed to appear at three races on the same day without having signed a contract for any of them.

Poulidor's agent was a tall man with fair hair, Roger Piel, a former rider who had three times been national pursuit champion on the track and who in 1946 came third in the world championship, held at Zurich. Seeing the way that riders had to deal with track managers who were better at business than they were, he tried negotiating on their behalf when his racing career ended. The stars told him they knew their worth and sent him away and he was left with the sideshow riders, their percentage giving him an income but not a fortune. And then he met Raymond Poulidor, an encounter so professionally advantageous that he called his autobiography "Merci, Poulidor!"

Anquetil and most of the other big riders were with Daniel Dousset. A few went to Piel because they didn't like Dousset or because they saw their interests elsewhere but, in shorthand, Dousset had the stars and Piel had the make-weights. Dousset was a professional one season before the Second World War and for two separate seasons (1946 and 1950) after it. He too had seen the chaos of promised, unsigned or forgotten track contracts. He was born in Paris in 1917 but he had the dark looks of a Corsican and a 100-word vocabulary that reminded many of a Mafia chief. He was no crook—everyone says he paid his bills honourably—but he was the ultimate Mr Ten Percent. He worked from a room behind his wife's bar near the Vélodrome d'Hiver.

Piel came on the scene in 1954 and a turf war broke out instantly. In the crossfire were the riders. As William Fotheringham put it: "It was a cartel. If a cyclist was not on one of the agents' books he had no appearance money: nothing to live off other than prize money and whatever his team might pay him. As a result, the agent-rider relationship was one of dependence on the rider's side, exploitation on that of the manager. Dousset or Piel could always find new riders; the riders had nowhere else to turn."[156]

Such was their importance and that of the post-Tour contracts that Dousset in particular influenced the result of the Tour de France. In 1959, the Tour was led by the temperamental Spanish climber, Federico Bahamontes. Anquetil and another French favourite, Roger Rivière, were in the French national team. A further Frenchman, Henry Anglade, was well placed in a regional team. The story is long and complicated but the essence is that Rivière and Anquetil rode against Anglade, as indeed they were entitled to, and helped Bahamontes, which they weren't. The crowd whistled Anquetil when he rode his lap of honour at the Parc des Princes because, although not yet understanding why, they realised he had not just thrown the race to a Spaniard but contrived to stop a Frenchman. It took a while but eventually the story emerged. Anglade was a bossy man and not much liked. Riders referred to him as "the colonel" or as Napoleon. That was enough to cut off any illicit help between teams. But more significant was that Anglade was with Roger Piel. It was because of that link, it was said, that he was denied a place in the national team alongside Dousset's clients.

Dousset turned up during the Tour and pointed out that it was much better that Bahamontes should win because he neither liked post-race criteriums—they were too fast for lightly-built climbers—nor racing outside Spain. He was therefore no threat to Anquetil or Rivière's start money and therefore to Dousset's percentage. Guimard realised straight away what was going on and he pointed out that it was surely no coincidence that Dousset had appeared on the scene. But what did Anquetil care about Anglade? Nothing. Nor about the insults as he rode round the Parc des Princes. He went home to his château with his winnings and bought a boat, which he named *Sifflets 59*—the whistles of '59.

Anglade stopped racing in 1968 and went into selling typewriters before becoming the manager of Lejeune, a team sponsored by a Paris bike factory, where his riders included Lucien van Impe and Ferdi Bracke. He later moved to Labastide d'Armagnac, near Mont-de-Marsan in the south-west, where he took up glass-staining and made windows for the Notre Dame des Cyclistes chapel outside the village.

Piel's and especially Dousset's grasp on the sport weakened and in time ended after the arrival of Renault as a team sponsor in 1978. Renault, a car and truck maker, was one of numerous companies which, like *L'Auto*, had been confiscated by the government after the war because of its collaboration with the Germans (something members of the family still dispute[157]) and it was still in government control. Its bosses, akin to civil servants and accustomed to more formal ways, asked the team manager, Cyrille Guimard, just who was employing the riders. Guimard explained the tricky position, that he was engaging them on behalf of Renault but that they were bound to an agency contract with Dousset or Piel. Renault wanted nothing of it and put the riders on its payroll along with every other employee. And for Dousset and Piel that broke two decades or more of living on a percentage of almost every high-earning rider in Europe.

There are still agents, of course, and they still take a percentage of contracts. But there are more of them and they work more conventionally and riders are directly employed by the sponsors or by a company set up, often by the team manager, to run its affairs. And the appearance races which once drew thousands to pay to stand on the streets of their own towns have now all but gone. The two old agents retired; Dousset died in 1997 and Roger Piel in 2002.

Anquetil resented that, no matter what he did, Poulidor remained more popular. As Poulidor was loved, so he was hated. The word is not an exaggeration so far as the more demonstrative *Poulidoristes* were concerned. Raphaël Géminiani, who managed Anquetil in the St-Raphaël and Ford teams, recalled: "There was real animosity towards Anquetil. I saw some shameful things. In the time-trials: crude gestures [*bras d'honneur*], insults, spitting, and in the mountains it was terrible."[158]

Poulidor disliked Anquetil for his aloofness and, though perhaps he would never have admitted it, because he kept preventing his winning the Tour de France. Anquetil was the more popular with the riders themselves, a gentlemen in business even though he didn't always remember their names. Such was his mental state about Poulidor that he once sent team-mates chasing after a harmless rider called Polidori because he couldn't face the headlines he knew would follow if he was beaten.

VOICES FROM THE PAST

[Anquetil was intrigued by riding a British time-trial] and he was keen to ride if he could get £1,000—in 1964, remember. He was asking what hills there would be and Tom Simpson, who was with us, assured him that the average British time-trial never rose more than 200 feet the whole way. And he said: "Well, that's no problem, then." I asked him what time he thought he would do for twenty-five miles. Bear in mind that he had no idea what [the national record] was. He said 46 minutes. The record was 54 minutes 23 seconds, to Bas Breedon. With no guidance, he had estimated 8 minutes off the competition record.

—Alan Gayfer, former editor of *Cycling*, 1993

Anquetil and Poulidor made an unbeatable couple in appearance races; if a promoter could afford both, and if they agreed to meet, he had the attraction of the year. Yet Poulidor was becoming more famous, more popular, more invited for losing than Anquetil was for winning. If Poulidor lost, it was because he was unlucky; if Anquetil won, it was because he was cold and scheming. One of the Tour's greatest moments came on the helter-skelter of the road that wound round and round the extinct volcano of the Puy-de-Dôme on 12 July 1964. Anquetil and Poulidor fought side by side until Anquetil cracked just before the summit to let Poulidor ride on alone. Anquetil crossed the line drained and for a moment thought he had lost the yellow jersey.

Three facts about that day show the difference between the two men, why one kept winning and the other did not. The first is that

Anquetil had allowed two climbers, Bahamontes and Julio Jimenez, to attack unchallenged and lead by themselves. That meant that Poulidor wouldn't take a time bonus even if he beat Anquetil, and it obliged Poulidor to stay with him in the strategic equivalent of the crocodile following Captain Hook. The second is that within seconds of staggering across the line, Anquetil asked what lead he still had overall. "Fourteen seconds," Géminiani told him. "Thirteen too many," Anquetil retorted, still breathing heavily. A single second would be enough. Once more, the moment portrayed him as a calculating robot.[159]

The third is that Poulidor admitted to his manager, Antonin Magne, that it could just as easily have been he who cracked on the mountain, because his bottom gear had been too high. Poulidor, far less a tactician, should have said nothing. Because when Magne unexpectedly asked about his test ride up the mountain before the race, Poulidor had to admit that he had driven there only to find that the road, which was private, was closed to visitors that day. Where Anquetil was a strategist, Poulidor was a blunderer. And yet by the time that Anquetil won that Tour in the closing time-trial, the crowd had sided with Poulidor.

Géminiani, who was still telling cycling stories in his nineties, came up with a plan to show for good which was the better. Anquetil, he said, would ride the hard Dauphiné Libéré stage race, beat Poulidor in the process, and then without a night's sleep fly to Bordeaux (in Charles de Gaulle's presidential jet, although it has never been formally confirmed) and then start the world's longest single-day race, 556 kilometres to Paris. And all without a night's sleep. Anquetil won. And did that set the record straight? No. People admired what he'd done—how could they not?—but, yes, yes, he must have done it on drugs. There probably wasn't a rider in the race who wouldn't have done the same and yet Anquetil had beaten them after coming straight from the Dauphiné Libéré.

Eventually he and Poulidor patched up their differences and became close enough friends that Anquetil, as he lay dying, could tease Poulidor that once more he would be second. The story is often denied, with explanations of why it could never have happened. There was a time when I, too, wasn't sure. And then I wrote to Poulidor and received a reply by return to say that, yes indeed, the story was true.

Anquetil rode his last races to public indifference, his very last appearance happening in Belgium because he was still cross at the way France had honoured the Belgian, Ferdi Bracke, for breaking his hour record without having been honoured himself. But few people cared. He had clung on too long and his views on doping, however honestly held, had become embarrassing. Poulidor, too, kept racing beyond his prime, and he was not unaware that it was only through being repeatedly beaten by Anquetil that he could make a happy living from personal appearances and endorsements for many years afterwards.

France has had glory days since then but never at the level of the decades after the war or the era of the *bande des copains* before it. Bernard Hinault gave the country fresh pride with his aggressive riding but he was hard to like. And Laurent Fignon, who also won the Tour—and spectacularly lost it one year by eight seconds to Greg Lemond—was seen as more of a technician than an idol.

The Tour kept Desgrange's initials on its yellow jersey and now and then there were shades of his quest for a superman. When riders went on strike and walked across the line at Valence d'Agen in the southwest in 1978, they had little sympathy from Goddet and Lévitan. The riders' anger at being shaken from their beds after the few hours of sleep allowed to them after a demanding mountain stage, just so the Tour could bring its accounts straight by having two stages in the same day, brought the retort from Goddet that "excess was necessary." We'll return to that story later.

Goddet was born in Paris on 21 June 1905. He stepped into his father's shoes, a newly-married man, when Victor died in 1926. But while he was the boss's son, he started at the bottom, learning to write as a newspaper needs. His role was assured when he persuaded Mussolini to talk to him in 1930 about his views on sport. Legend says he always declined to take the lift to his office on the fourth floor of the new offices at Issy-le-Moulineaux, climbing the stairs for the exercise they gave him—further shades of Desgrange. "I don't mind old age," he used to say—he died at ninety-five—"it's a privilege. The only trouble is that it doesn't last long."

Goddet was educated in Britain, near Oxford but not at the university as legend has it. He remembered bike rides in the Thames valley—ended by an arm broken at rugby—and kept a fondness for Britain and the British that he nevertheless didn't flaunt. In his early years he promoted the few English-speaking journalists however minor to being "from *The Times.*" It was a flattery that didn't extend to his notorious press officer, Louis Lapeyre, who refused to speak to any of them, let alone in English.

Goddet took his literary lead from Desgrange. He wrote not of the end of stages but of *les arrivées magistrales*. Louison Bobet, slower one day than expected, had gallantly accepted "the delay attributed to him by the celestial handicapper." Where, in Geoffrey Nicholson's words, most journalists on the Tour dressed as though they had just crawled out of a foxhole, Goddet was immaculate in khaki shorts and shirt, knee-length socks, putting on a colonial pith helmet in the south and peering through his car roof like a tank captain. I asked him once about the helmet. "It was just chance the first time I did it," he said, "but when it proved popular I did it every year. It was certainly cooler and it added colour to the race." I also asked him what he made of the race that he had organised for so many years but which had changed so much since. He didn't say he approved, nor that he disapproved.

"Everything must change," he growled.

He was ninety-two, a little short of hearing, his voice rough, and his skin sagging like a dachshund's. But he was tall and unbent. "Without change, progress is impossible," he continued. He was always the master of the enigmatic, Goddet; like Bob Dylan's lyrics, you think you've understood and then you realise that perhaps you hadn't, that there must have been something you missed.

This was, nevertheless, the man who enjoyed imposing the risks and extremes of the violent cobbles of Paris–Roubaix, which he described in approving tones as cycling's last folly. Maybe he thought cycling had grown soft. Certainly Desgrange would have thought so. Goddet and Desgrange sent riders over the impossible, whatever the road or climate. If the going wasn't tough enough, they made it tougher. It's not always that way now. I stayed once with a man who that morning had ridden out to watch Paris–Nice. He and others stood in falling snow and waited. Perhaps their memories were wrapped in the days of legend, when Charly Gaul had to be carried frozen off his bike on a mountain top, or when the Tour ploughed a furrow between banks of snow.

Maybe, too, they remembered a more recent race, the Liège–Bastogne–Liège of 1980, when a polar wind whipped and snow fell as the race left Liège. Spectators stood like snowmen. Within an hour some teams had barely a man left. The abandonments averaged a man a minute for the first hour. In the same race in 1957, rider after rider disappeared for warmth into roadside bars. The giant Frenchman, Gérard Saint, stopped to piss on his hands to bring them back to life.

And what happened that day my friend had ridden through the snow to see Paris–Nice? They saw the riders, certainly. But they were all sitting in buses.

Desgrange would never have countenanced that. The only way to find a superman, he believed, was to set super-tasks. And that's what he did. But super-tasks bring super-solutions. And cyclists have been no less ingenious than other athletes. Desgrange knew about drug-taking and, never having spoken out about it publicly, or at least to any extent, he can be assumed to have tolerated or even accepted it. He died, though, before the amphetamine era. Chemists isolated Benzedrine between the world wars and it went on sale in 1933 as a nasal decongestant. Three years later a development of Benzedrine went on sale to treat obesity, low blood pressure, and even a disappointing sex life.[160] It was, in short, a miracle drug and many sports bodies correspondingly viewed it without criticism.

Millions of Benzedrine tablets were handed to airmen and soldiers during the war, on all sides—British troops got through seventy-two million of them—and warehouses of surplus stock were sold off after 1945. The drug swamped not just endurance sports but many in which at first sight it wasn't useful. It provided excitement and self-confidence. It became known as speed, and that was its attraction in cycling. As early as 1948, Dr Christopher Woodard was saying in *Cycling* and *The Bicycle* that he was "very suspicious that some competitors [in a world championship] were receiving artificial stimulants, and it is my opinion that this drug-taking by others was a very large factor in our not achieving Olympic or world honours this year." He enlarged on that in the *New York Times* on 1 October 1948: "I was able to see things at closer range at the world cycling championships in Amsterdam, where I spent some of my time on the inside of the track. Few other than our own [British] team knew who I was. Imagine my surprise, therefore, when a garrulous foreigner surreptitiously tried to show me his pet concoction of strychnine, caffeine and Benzedrine."

Woodard was an odd character who had his own column in cycling papers and wrote a training manual which gave little advice beyond eccentrically promising success to riders who drank neither tea nor coffee.[161] He enjoyed his position as an authority in a sport in which few medical people showed any interest. There was great excitement when the American president, Dwight Eisenhower, had a heart attack in 1955, not because of the attack but because his doctor, Paul White, urged him to ride a bicycle.[162] It was celebrity at a very distant step but gratefully received when there was so little else. So far as drugs were concerned, though, Woodard was both well-intentioned and right.

It's hard in this era of power meters, heart monitors and the like to imagine just how in the dark cyclists used to be in even our own lifetimes. They believed that miles made the man, that the more you rode, the better you would be. That, to an extent, was true. But it exhausted as much as it extended. And because of that, riders left their bikes untouched for three months at the end of the season in the belief that their bodies and brains needed the break. The consequences at the start of the new year were predictable and bloody.

A coach, Bill James, wrote in *Sporting Cyclist*: "I wince now when I think of some of the get-fit ideas I followed as a teenager. One such bash stands out in mind, the annual Corfe Castle run. There and back in the same day—230 miles, on fixed [gear], of course. The last thirty miles or so were virtually done in an insensitive daze, but since the big boys—Fleming, Walter, Burgess, Pond, Hill—did this, you did not question why."

We can piece together when that must have been. Lew Pond, whom he mentions, died only in 2014, having continued to ride a bike into his nineties; George Fleming, the first man in Britain to ride a fifty-mile time-trial in less than two hours, died in 1997; Gerry Burgess, who died in 1999, was a national tandem champion with Pond and a maker of pioneering alloy cycle components in the 1960s. This wasn't cycling pre-history, when men wore moustaches and Britain owned India: it was of our times.

The British, it has to be said, were obsessive even for the age and Francis Pélissier—brother of Charles and Henri—was horrified to hear the training routines of a handful of British cyclists who made it to his training camp in Monaco in the late 1950s; until then they'd been riding 100 miles on both Saturday and Sunday—"ridiculous"—and then as far as they could manage after work during the week. The British, in turn, were surprised to find that what they had expected to be a week of day-long tear-ups turned out to be gentle half-day promenades followed by a sleep.

British cycling had been isolated from world cycling for sixty years because of its own internal politics—the national body banned road-racing from 1888 until a rebel body forced it to change direction in the 1950s—and therefore the bikes that British riders used at world championships in the 1930s were a matter of considerable interest for their eccentricity. Percy Stallard, an early rider on the continent, trained in a khaki shirt and shorts and was nicknamed Boy Scout because of it. When Britain organised the world road-race championship in 1922, it ran it in secret, as a time-trial and with the British riders, at least, dressed from neck to toe in black as time-trialling regulations then required.[163]

There are reports in *Cycling* of British riders calling for "stimulants", and the German paper, *Rad Welt,* said: "The English amateurs were full of [drugs]. Owen and Oakes are said to have ridden as if drunk, and all the other amateurs showed every indication that they had also taken dope."

Cycling was a sport of tradition, mumbo-jumbo whispered between riders and above all their soigneurs, the holders of the secrets. It probably doesn't matter if the word *soigneur* came from or passed into boxing. In boxing, he is the second, the man who in other times had a "da's my boy" manner and the job of keeping his man upright and fighting after he perhaps should have stopped. In cycling and boxing alike, soigneurs were a cross between knowledgeable old practitioners and outright charlatans. Anything went. Pierre Chany wrote of them: "They are often colourful, sometimes doubtful, part of the folklore of the race. They are very aware of their importance. There was Pierre Viel, their flag-carrier, Joseph Torcin with his cigar, old Giuseppe Leoni with his mumbo-jumbo mixture of French and Italian, Léon Sonnet, Guerlache, etc."[164]

Jean-Pierre de Mondenard, a French doctor with an unparalleled knowledge of the history of doping, mocked their far-from-medical backgrounds: "Pompously called soigneurs, their professional origins had only the most distant link with medicine. In this rag-bag brotherhood, we find a teacher of panel-beating (for Bernard Vallet), a wine salesman (for Sean Kelly), a chauffeur (for Jacques Anquetil), an insurance agent (for Bernard Thévenet), a newspaper delivery man and bus driver (for Richard Virenque), several former riders and even a pastry cook (for Bernard Hinault)."[165] Of the British team in the 1967 Tour de France, Vin Denson was looked after by Bernard Stoops, who away from cycling was a gravedigger, and Colin Lewis by a fishmonger.[166]

William Fotheringham says: "These *eminences grises* traded on their mystique, their secret remedies, their little tricks handed down from generation to generation, some of which still survive. It is impossible to define how much they actually delivered, how much was common sense and basic science, and how much was trickery designed to make the cyclists feel they were in possession of something—a drug, a dietary secret, a way of training—which their fellows did not have." He quotes Harry Hall, the British team's mechanic, saying of Gus Naessens, who was Tom Simpson's soigneur in 1967, that "he used to buy cattle feed and boil it like a witch's brew in the hotel kitchen, then put it in the [riders'] bottles. It was so heavy, like thick rice pudding, that when they were handed up in the bags at the feed they would break the bags."[167] Naessens' theory was that it would dissolve slowly in the stomach and keep riders going while sparing them the effort of contracting their stomach muscles to digest more conventional food.

Willem van Wijnendaele, a Belgian journalist and the founder of the Tour of Flanders, wrote in 1954 of Leandro Faggin, an Italian pursuiter, being in "a shocking state half an hour before his ride against the general favourite… His feverish eyes were deep into his face and he kept licking his dry lips as though he had a thirst but nothing to help it. They were signs that no doctor could mistake and we all knew that he had taken something. I pointed him out to several colleagues and in no time there was a crowd of soigneurs, journalists and managers, all having a look. Someone shouted: 'Nobody smoke in case there's an explosion.'"[168]

Deaths began to be attributed to Benzedrine and other amphetamines. The 23-year-old Danish rider, Knut Enemark Jensen, died in the Olympic team time-trial in Rome in 1960. There is some dispute whether doping was a cause or a contribution[169] but the Dutch official, Dr Piet van Dijk, said of Rome that "Prominent officials have assured me that dope had never been used in such royal quantities as it was in Rome." The sport knew it was happening—how could it not know if it was that widespread?—but it kept a silence. There was no rule against it.

Desgrange never had to bother with dope controls. Indeed, when he brought in national teams in 1930 he told the national federations and their riders, according to Benjo Maso in *Het zweet der goden*, that he would pay for their hotels and food but not for their stimulants, as drugs were then called. Dope tests started hesitantly in 1965 after Jensen's death started to change attitudes. Drugs were so ingrained and the controls so easily cheated, that the British team manager Alex Taylor said he had seen "the over-cautious way riders were tested for dope, as if the authorities feared to lift the veil, scared of how to handle the results, knowing all the while what they would be. They let the show carry on while the law acted light-heartedly, without vigour and purpose—and its deterrent had no effect."[170]

It has to be said that some self-serving is going on here. Taylor was no stranger to continental racing, having been born and having raced in Belgium, having himself been a professional for four years and, above all, having been the British team manager when Tom Simpson died in a British jersey with Union Jacks on its shoulders in 1967. If he didn't know what was going on in the Tour generally—he had already seen the "over-cautious" tests, remember—and if he didn't know what was going on with his team leader specifically, then he hadn't been doing his job. Nevertheless, he told me in late 1967, when he lived in a mobile home in Puckeridge north of London that "a team manager doesn't see everything." We'll return in more detail to Simpson's story, not because he was a lone offender—far from it—but because his death in the quest for supermanhood was so striking and, being cycling, provoked a nevertheless slow and reluctant change of attitude within the sport.

Specialist journalists whose access to riders depended on not spitting in the soup, as the sport called it, knew as much as the riders but spoke of it even less. But Simpson's death in 1967 prompted a London journalist called Jim Manning to step where his specialist colleagues had avoided. A week after Simpson's death, when British cyclists preferred to think Simpson had died of foolish courage and when the British Cycling Federation met in private and declined to organise an inquiry, he wrote in the *Daily Mail*: "Is France trying to hush up the scandals of the Tour? I say yes. The first act of hushing up is not to attempt detection, let alone waiting a year before taking action. How much husher can you get?

"Three days after this year's race, the French authorities announced that next October and November a French and Italian rider would be prosecuted for alleged doping offences in last year's Tour. France has surrendered the need rigorously to prevent doping to the discreet requirement of not tackling it on a big tourist occasion until a year had passed safely. That is my accusation: I nail it firmly to the wall. It takes two days at most to analyse samples; it took a year for France to authorise prosecutions. What devious explanation can be expected?"

Manning also wrote: "Tommy Simpson rode to his death in the Tour de France so doped that he did not know he had reached the limit of his endurance. He died in the saddle, slowly asphyxiated by intense effort in a heatwave after taking methyl-amphetamine drugs and alcoholic stimulants."[171] It was the first time that British cyclists, perhaps all cyclists, had been so rudely jolted with a truth they still doubted. Manning had no respect for sports "non-journalists", a remark that obliged him to pay £300 damages to the compilers of the *Guinness Book of Records,* whom he particularly disliked.[172]

There *had* been dope tests—the first, at Bordeaux, had provoked riders to get off and walk and nothing was ever heard of the results—but they were dissuasive rather than conclusive. They detected only some amphetamines—specifically Maxiton and Tonédron—and only then if they were taken in quantities sufficient for a horse.[173] Simpson either had no fear of dope tests or he was prepared to trick them because his pockets contained a tube of Tonédron tablets when he died.

Cycling had no choice but to wring its hands and act. Riders tried to give their protests a respectable edge by insisting that banning amphetamines would bring more serious drugs in their wake. And sure enough it did, because both medicine and human ingenuity advanced. Cycling tested for steroids for the first time at the 1978 world championship and the Swiss rider, Gilbert Glaus, became the first to be caught. That was embarrassing for him but it was significant for cycling. Steroids and their like had been in sport since 1938 but interest in them vanished when the results were inconclusive and when, anyway, the world had other things on its mind: it went to war next year. A few summers after the war, legend says, California beach boys rediscovered the drug and blessed it for giving them bulkier and more impressive bodies. Rumour had it that the Russians had already noticed that and that they were experimenting. That rumour reached John Ziegler, a big, fleshy physician and former marine who treated American Olympic athletes, and he worked with the Swiss company, CIBA, to give the drug to weightlifters. He was himself a weight-trainer.

Ziegler says he noticed—he could hardly ignore—how much bulkier Russian competitors were at the world weightlifting championship in 1954 and, he says, he got a drunk Russian trainer to tell him that his team was taking testosterone. Ineffective results back at Ziegler's club in York, Pennsylvania, were followed by CIBA's research and the marketing of Dianabol.[174] Pink Dianabol pills ran riot through sport. When it wasn't used to put on bulk, it and its derivatives were used to repair muscle damage and allow harder and more frequent training. That was its attraction to cycling. The names and varieties of drugs are bewildering but here the point is that for the first time riders were able to take drugs that helped them not just in a single race but, as a course, for a whole season. And it worked as well off-season as during training.

VOICES FROM THE PAST

I took him along to a training camp in Spain. The boy changed then into a sort of lion. He raced as though he was powered by rockets… I went to talk to him. He was really happy he was riding so well and he told me to look out for him. I asked him if he perhaps wasn't "using something" and he jumped straight up, climbed on a chair, and from deep inside a closet pulled out a plastic bag of pills. I felt my heart skip a beat. With a soigneur and another rider, we counted the pills. There were five thousand of them, excluding hormone preparations and sleeping pills. I took the five thousand bombs, to his own relief. I let him keep the hormones and sleeping pills. Later he seemed to have taken too many at once and he slept for a couple of days on end. We couldn't wake him up. We took him to hospital and they pumped out his stomach. They tied him to his bed to prevent anything going wrong again. But somehow he had taken some stimulant and fancied taking a walk. A nurse came across him in the corridor walking along with the bed strapped to his back.

—Dutch team manager Kees Pellenaars, *Daar was't*, 1973

VOICES FROM THE PAST

I take stimulants. It's impossible, as a professional, to do otherwise. But my advice to you young riders is not to do the same.

—Jacques Anquetil, *L'Humanité*, 22 October 1967

VOICES FROM THE PAST

[He asked me if I had "prepared"] I showed him my bike and let him check my tyres. To my surprise he shook his head. He didn't mean that at all. He meant whether I had taken anything.

"How do you mean, taken?"

"Good Lord," he said. He took me along to his cabin and opened a case. "What do you think?" he asked. It looked just like a chemist's shop. Pills, powders, everything.

"Here," he said.

"Stenamine," I read.

"Take it."

I swallowed and in a flash I was in heaven. I felt I could fly. I only had to stick out my wings and I'd be away. I rode fantastically. If doctors say now that stuff doesn't do anything, I just have to laugh. The spectators were really enthusiastic and I got a contract for fifteen races.

—Theo Sijthoff in *25 Jaar Doping*, 1974

10
Mountain unclimbed

The last ride that Tom Simpson made was from the village of Bédoin in eastern France towards the top of the mountain from which the village makes its living. Unless you are a naturist visiting the campsite there, there is little other reason to go than to try your hand on Mont Ventoux. Hundreds of nameless cyclists do it every weekend. At one end of the slope through the small town is a bike shop that sells socks embroidered with the mountain's name. At the other are a succession of bars and restaurants. Cyclists sit outside many of them, happy to have reached the top of the mountain or wondering whether to put off climbing it until another day.

One of those bars is the Observatoire, named after the astronomy centre at the mountain's peak. The café has red awnings, a spread of tables and cushioned wooden chairs outside and, above the awnings, three wide windows set in brown wooden frames, slightly inset and curved at the top. There is nothing there to say so but it was from that bar that Tom Simpson got his last illicit drink of the 1967 Tour de France. He had set out after a disappointing season the previous year to show he was the superman that his British fans believed him to be and because, more prosaically, Daniel Dousset had told him his contract price would be hopeless if he didn't make a name in the Tour. "He set out that year to win the Tour de France," his wife Helen said in a BBC radio documentary twenty years after the day.

In the middle of 13 July 1967, Colin Lewis arrived at Bédoin beside Simpson, his leader and room-mate. He knew that Simpson wouldn't be in his company much longer. Simpson was a practised professional, Lewis a weekend part-timer back home in Devon and, effectively, riding the Tour de France in his holidays. His job that day was to run Simpson's errands, which in Bédoin meant raiding the Observatoire for whatever he could steal. He joined the other riders in their plunder and came out with a bottle of Coca-Cola and four others he hadn't had time to check. It wasn't his first raid. A photo of the same Tour caught his Condor bike lying on the road outside a bar from which other riders were escaping with their booty.[175]

"I stuffed three of them into my back pocket and the other down the back of my neck," he remembered. "Out of the bar, I worked my way through the convoy and back to the peloton. Tom was my major concern and I gave him the Coca-Cola, which he was really pleased about. He took a long drink and handed it to the next guy."[176] Simpson asked what else Lewis had. Out came a small bottle of brandy. Simpson said it would help settle his stomach and he took a swig and threw the bottle over a hedge and into a field of sunflowers.

Go to the Observatoire now and they will tell you the story, the *chasse à la canette* and its circumstances, the significance of which they found out only later. Many reports say it was Simpson himself who raided the bar but that was confusion of white jerseys with their Union Jack on the shoulder and because for the rest of the year Simpson rode in the white jersey of the Peugeot team. Stars didn't do the dirty work themselves. Just as when van Looy ordered Vin Denson to find him a café, they got their lesser riders to do their bidding for them. Had Simpson stopped then, in all probability the others would have attacked. He wasn't an obvious contender for the overall victory but they would miss no chance to push him down the list.

Simpson was adventurous in races, often beyond the point of rashness. But his light build made him best at races up to a week, whereas the Tour lasted a month. He was light enough to ride wheels with twenty-eight spokes, usually chosen for the track, where others preferred thirty-six. That lightness was an advantage on long but not devastating climbs like Mont Ventoux. It is 22 kilometres from Bédoin to the observatory 1,622 metres higher, though the first kilometres rise only gently. The rest is steep and grinding, with ramps of nearly eleven per cent. The problem in summer is the heat, because for two thirds of its rise it passes through fly-ridden woods that hog the air. Doubtless with colour and imagination thrown in for the same price, Antoine Blondin, the most literary of cycling writers, wrote: "There are few happy memories of this sorcerer's cauldron. We have seen riders reduced to madness under the effect of the heat or stimulants, some coming back down the hairpin they thought they were climbing, others brandishing their pumps and accusing us of murder… falling men, tongues hanging out, selling their soul for a drop of water, a little shade."

Whether riders or anyone else took that story seriously, they all knew that a French rider, Jean Malléjac, had collapsed on the mountain in 1955 and been put in an ambulance with his legs still pedalling a bike that was no longer there. He was "streaming with sweat, haggard and comatose, zigzagging, and the road wasn't wide enough for him," the Tour archivist, Jacques Augendre, remembered.

Malléjac never denied that he was drugged, only that he had drugged himself. The dope had perhaps been in a bottle handed up by a soigneur, he thought in a television interview two days before Simpson's death.[177] Other riders were less cynical. If they needed drugs to get up Mont Ventoux, at racing speed for the front men or simply to get up at all for the rest, then many of them would take them. It was in the culture. They just hoped they'd be luckier than Malléjac.

VOICES FROM THE PAST

You would have to be naive or a hypocrite to insist that the Tour de France, Bordeaux–Paris, Dauphiné Libéré, can be ridden on just mineral water… All the riders take something.

—Jacques Anquetil in a television debate with François Misoffe, the sports minister, 1967

VOICES FROM THE PAST

Personally, I take stimulants and I don't hide it. But people lump it all together—drugs, doping and stimulants—without knowing what they mean. All riders need stimulants.

—Jacques Anquetil, *Miroir Sprint*, 9 May 1966

Simpson said of Mont Ventoux that "it is like another world up there among the bare rocks and the glaring sun… I think it was the only time that I have got off my bike and my pants have nearly fallen down. They were soaked and heavy with sweat which was running off me in streams and I had to wring out my socks because the sweat was running into my shoes."[178]

Twenty kilometres after swigging his brandy, Simpson lay white and inert by the roadside. He had fallen once, got back on and struggled a little further before Harry Hall, the mechanic, ran from his car and grabbed him before he rode groggily off the side of the unprotected road and into the ravine. The Tour's doctor, Pierre Dumas, who for some years had led an international protest against drug-taking, clamped an oxygen mask over Simpson's face. One of the two police helicopters escorting the Tour landed at 4:40 p.m. to take Simpson away. It looked, said a television commentator, like a black vulture as it turned and flew off towards Avignon. In it, Dumas's assistant, Ferrocio Macorig, took turns with a nurse in massaging Simpson's heart.

Simpson's jersey held three small tubes, two empty and one labelled as containing Tonédron. Dumas felt them in his pockets as he began lifting Simpson's jersey to bare his chest for heart massage. He took them out at the hospital and gave them to the police team that had started to gather. Police found more drugs in Simpson's luggage.

VOICES FROM THE PAST

We had heard that Tom was up with the leaders climbing the Ventoux. Then as we accelerated ahead down the tricky descent ahead of Jimenez, the reports began to come through again with no mention of Tom. Only when we reached the finish to await the riders did we learn that he had fallen, assuming it was a crash. Then the team car came in and we knew that he had collapsed, but still with no inkling that the end was to be so tragic… Gradually the rumours grew, defying belief, until we had the official announcement.

—Sid Saltmarsh, *Cycling*, 22 July 1967

Dirty Feet

The autopsy decided that Simpson had died of heart failure caused by exhaustion, dehydration and heat. The report added that "the amount of amphetamine that Simpson took could not have killed him by itself but it could have led him to go beyond his limits."[179] It was just that that Jim Manning had written. The British Cycling Federation racing secretary, Bryan Wotton, said so many calls came into the offices in sedate Park Crescent on the edge of London's Regent's Park that there was no time to think of anything else, let alone an inquiry. The autopsy records in France were filed, the case closed and the paperwork eventually thrown away.

VOICES FROM THE PAST

A champion, he wanted victory too badly, with all that it could bring to his happiness as a father and husband. We often asked ourselves if this athlete, who at work so often appeared in pain, had not committed some errors in the way he looked after himself. Doping? We can fear the public revelation of a tragedy caused by this scourge.

—Jacques Goddet, *L'Équipe*, 14 July 1967

More than half a century after his death, Simpson still rides the races of old men's memories. There are websites and internet discussion groups in his memory. Advertising a film in which Simpson appears guarantees an audience. To modern riders he is as distant as miniskirts, radio stations on the North Sea and teenagers who said "fab" and "groovy." Even *Cycling Weekly* (or just plain *Cycling* as it was in Simpson's day) can't bring itself to acknowledge what he achieved. He is remembered not for his victories but for the day of his death and the way it revealed him, along with the sport in which he made his living, as a drug-taker. It named not Simpson as its man of the century in 2001 but the track rider Chris Boardman, breaker of the world hour record but never once a finisher in the Tour de France nor a world champion on the road. The debate filled the magazine's letters pages for weeks, as no doubt the magazine hoped.

Simpson is remembered now by the memorial on the mountain and by a little-known museum in the Harworth village of Nottinghamshire where he was buried beneath a black marble stone that carries the message "His body ached, his legs grew tired, but still he would not give in." Nearby is the Harworth and Bircotes sports club and, in it, a small collection of Simpson memorabilia. His white Peugeot bike is there, though not the one he rode in the Tour but the one on which he won Paris–Nice in 1965, along with his Tour de France white jersey with its Union Jack on each shoulder. It's when you see that jersey, and those kept by his friend Vin Denson, that you understand how shallow-chested Simpson was. "We often used to laugh at Tom in the showers," Denson says, convinced that his pigeon chest was the result of generations of mining and marvelling that it could ever have held enough air.[180]

There are front pages of newspapers. The *Daily Mirror* announces "Cycling ace Tommy dies in the cruel sun" in capitals with a long thin picture of Simpson's face, haggard and drawn, as he nears the top of the climb. Opposite it, a smaller picture shows Pierre Dumas struggling to bring him back to life. The *Daily Express*, then still a broadsheet, also leads with the story. Its headline over four columns announces "Heat kills cycle ace" over a single-column picture of Simpson riding towards the camera. More personal and because of it more moving is the log book of Harry Hall, the mechanic first on the scene with his colleague Ken Ryall when Simpson collapsed. In it he has hurriedly pencilled in the size of the sprockets on the back wheel that he fitted the previous night to get his man over the mountain. "Ventoux: 14/15/17/19/22/23" he has written, followed by his summary of the general state of the bike: "Rest OK."

The soigneurs justified their presence, and in turn the riders said they needed their help, by the inhuman distances that the Tour imposed. Ordinary men were being asked to become supermen—which Desgrange had wanted since the start—but it was impossible. It was impossible even to finish the race without doping. In which case, clearly, there was something wrong with the controls. Jacques Goddet said in 1999, after his retirement: "I feel real resentment towards the medical and scientific powers who have deceived us for thirty years. There were 107 controls in the 1998 Tour [when the police arrested and charged riders who subsequently confessed to taking drugs, and when a trial established that there had been systematic doping]—and they were all negative. The controls are almost always negative, which means that the labs have been making serious mistakes, mistakes that have only served to speed up the growth of this evil. The controls that we developed after Simpson's death were a lie, covered up by the highest scientific and medical authorities."

He didn't go into detail.

VOICES FROM THE PAST

We had the privilege on Saturday evening of attending a dinner for winners of the Tour de France… One table particularly attracted attention: that of Anquetil, Merckx and Bobet, thirteen victories in the Tour between them. The conversation on the table was particularly lively and Louison Bobet was taken to task for daring to say that he had never taken the slightest stimulant or tonic. He was obliged to admit "that he had swallowed the contents of small bottles prepared by his soigneur at the time without knowing exactly what they contained." Which made Jacques Anquetil and Eddy Merckx laugh.

—Jean Leulliot, *Sud-Ouest,* 24 July 1978

William Fotheringham described the conflict of interest, pointing out that Goddet had been both organiser and reporter of the Tour, profiting from both, that he had described an exhausting stage over the Aubisque col as "a fabulous day" and that he had revelled in the "pitiless cruelty of cycling, a sport of total effort." He continued: "The Tour had been founded in 1903 in order to make headlines and sell newspapers by turning the participants into supermen who managed feats beyond mere mortals. That was no longer the overt message, as it had been in 1903, but Goddet and Lévitan were still at the same time creating the Tour route and profiting from the headlines and sales the superhuman feats in the race brought to their papers. Nowadays, that would be seen as a conflict of interest."[181]

Other voices also spoke to justify their position, often with further self-interest. The Dutchman Charles Ruys, a failed race organiser and a regular in *Cycling* if not always consistently coherent, turned up again under the headline "Desgranges [*sic*] yesterday—dope today."[182] The headline was more succinct than his article, which argued erratically that the road and certainly mountains were no place for racing cyclists. Their place was on the track, which would blossom and draw crowds if only it got the publicity that road racing enjoyed. He neglected to mention a few things: that he had only recently been part of a team organising road races in Holland, out of which he had been eased because he wasn't up to it; that he had helped manage a professional road team but hadn't been asked back; and that he had just become race director of the London six-day, where he hoped (but failed) to renew his contract.

> VOICES FROM THE PAST
>
> The road is not built for our sport, and most certainly not the roads over mountains. These obstacles are "imported" into our sport by men who wanted something different. They are as alien to bike-racing as Eskimos to the Sahara. The main culprit in my mind was Henri Desgranges [*sic*], the father of the Tour de France. His aim was to create a tough stage race in his country, so tough that, if he was lucky, only one man would be able to finish the race.
>
> —Charles Ruys, *Cycling*, 26 August 1967

Such false and self-interested tears weren't unusual in the third quarter of 1967. They included the hand-wringing of Alec Taylor, who had no idea of what Simpson was up to. And even more outrageous was the claim of the Frenchman, Maurice de Muer, who managed the Peugeot and Bic teams. Between 1970 and 1978, riders in his teams alone logged up twenty-four of the seventy positive dope tests. In 1977 he made his riders sign a waiver discharging him and his officials of responsibility in doping cases. His explanation was that he didn't have "eyes in the back of [his] head to watch riders 24 hours a day."[183] This in a period in which cycling was supposed to have learned the lesson of Simpson's death.

Dirty Feet

The 1967 Tour that Simpson rode as his last was 4,779 kilometres long. Few Tours since the war had been longer. The 1968 Tour, symbolically starting from Vittel, a town in the Vosges that trades on being the home of pure mountain water, was advertised as the Tour of Health. That didn't stop the former world champion, Jean Stablinski, being caught. There was no shortage of cynics to suggest that there was more advertising for mineral water than any serious expectation of change in cycling.

As an aside, and to confirm that false hope, Michel Pollentier was caught trying to defraud a control with a condom of urine and a long plastic tube after he won the stage to Alpe d'Huez in 1978. It says even more of the atmosphere in professional cycling that Pollentier's roommate and friend, Freddy Maertens, insists that the doctor would never have uncovered the trickery had he not been tipped off by the team's own manager, Fred De Bruyne. De Bruyne, according to Maertens, took a hefty bribe to ruin his own leader's chances, which helped him build a retirement villa in the south of France.

> VOICES FROM THE PAST
>
> You think I was the first?
>
> —Michel Pollentier, TF1 television, 16 July 1978

The UCI, the international body, tackled the wrong end of the problem after 1967 by limiting the length of races and imposing the number of rest days. The wrong end of the problem because it was easier to suggest that it was the distance that obliged riders to take drugs—the argument that the riders themselves used—than to tackle the problem itself: that drugs had been ingrained in cycling since the nineteenth century and that few people had felt inclined to say so or do anything about it.

The error of the distance argument was proved within weeks of the Tour's finish. Track racing is over a tiny distance compared to the road and, as Ruys pointed out, it doesn't involve going up hills, let alone mountains. It doesn't even involve riding in the rain. But a guilt-enthused flurry of tests caught rider after rider at the 1967 track world championships in Amsterdam. Out in the first week went the motor-paced riders Alex Boeye, Dieter Kemper, Freddy Ruegg and Kevin Crowe, and the Belgian all-rounder Yvonne Reynders. The second week turfed out two 200-metre sprinters (Ron Baensch and Walter Heberle), an amateur 4,000-metre pursuiter (Milan Przla) and the professional 5,000-metre pursuiter Charly Grosskost. None of them would have ridden more than an hour and the sprinters only for a dozen seconds. And that after René Chesal, the secretary of the UCI, said: "This will be the first guaranteed dope-free world cycling championship, of that we can be sure."[184] Or maybe that's what he meant: that there would be a list of disqualifications every week.

Grosskost was an especially colourful case, one of the few riders ever to be pushed off his bike for his own sake. As Christophe Penot wrote in *La France Cycliste,* the magazine of the French cycling federation: "He started as favourite in the Tour de l'Avenir [the abbreviated version of the Tour de France for amateurs and semi-professionals]. But had he 'prepared' himself too much? Or, to be clearer, had he swallowed too many amphetamines in an era when doping was a matter for riders' consciences rather than a matter for lawyers? The truth is that in that month of July 1965, ten years after Mallejac and two years before Tom Simpson, Grosskost was found on the road with his hands drawn across himself in a cross."[185] Did that discourage anyone? Hardly. The following year he turned pro. And for whom? Peugeot.

Charles de Gaulle preferred to look away. When Jacques Anquetil said no thinking professional would ride without stimulants, the response of the president was to shrug and say: "Doping? *Connais pas.* All I know is that he's a champion who made them play the Marseillaise."[186] Anquetil's position was honest and the only thing that distinguished him was that he spoke about doping openly. Pierre Chany said: "Jacques had the strength—for which he was always criticised—to say out loud what others would only whisper. So, when I asked him 'What have you taken?', he didn't drop his eyes before replying. He had the strength of conviction."[187]

Anquetil's argument was that cycling was a job. He had started racing not because he liked it but because it was a good way to meet girls. He never did enjoy it, always saw it as a means to an end, and when he retired he rode his bike just three more times, one of those into his swimming pool to amuse guests. If, he said, a teacher could take aspirin to quell a headache during a lesson then a professional cyclist could take something to deaden his own pain. That he couldn't, he said, was hypocrisy. Sadly for him, public sentiment moved away from him, pushed along by the cold shyness of his personality.

Goddet said Simpson's death was a reason he made later Tours shorter. But that just made riders race faster and more often. Henri Pélissier, who complained to Albert Londres of the inhuman demands made of him, rode just 33 races a year. Bernard Vallet, the best climber of the 1982 Tour, said he rode 225 in 1985, a rise of 750 per cent. In the eighteen years of his career, Pélissier raced 52,000 kilometres; fifty years later, Eddy Merckx rode 400,000 kilometres in just thirteen seasons.[188] Merckx, found positive three times, would have been banned for life under later rules.

Goddet wasn't unaware of what was going on. In his understated way, he had written of Simpson: "A champion, he wanted victory too badly... we often asked ourselves if this athlete, who at work often appeared in pain, had not committed some errors in his manner of looking after himself."[189] When it came to the Tour's interests, though, those of the organisers and accountants counted more than the "errors" of riders.

Goddet was the romantic who knew everyone in Paris society and Lévitan was the unashamed capitalist, selling every inch of bare space to an advertiser, any advertiser. The two got on less as the years passed and as they grew older and set in their ways, their coldness to each other towards the end hidden by public expressions of "*Mon cher Jacques*" and "*Mon cher Félix*." They had grand dreams but small ideas. Under them, the Tour became vibrant but even more so it became so sordid that there were serious suggestions it should be given to the state as part of the national heritage. Nobody expected that to happen but still less did they anticipate what happened next: that Lévitan would stand up, with Goddet's at least tacit support, and say that not only were the five-dime sponsors necessary but there must be many more.

One way the Tour made money was to sell starts and finishes to towns prepared to host them, as we saw at Valence d'Agen. It then, for several years, sold the rights for Europe-1, a radio station, to hold big and noisy street parties that drew boozy crowds to see France's biggest stars. Little thought was paid to the riders, who often stayed at small hotels in town centres within bass-thumping range of the loudspeakers. When the street parties ended, it wasn't for concern for the riders and their sleep, it was because Lévitan and Goddet feared they were becoming too popular and distracting from their race.

And so it was with selling starts and finishes to towns anxious for the publicity and trade. If a town wouldn't pay for both then the answer was simple: pack the riders into a bus after the finish and drive them off to whichever town would pay for a start. That has become more common in recent Tours, accelerated by the UCI's limit on the overall length of the race, but at the same time, the care taken of riders is better. They often travel by plane or in a chartered, air-conditioned trains.

And so we return in more detail to the Tour's first strike, at Valence d'Agen in 1978. Lévitan's grasping led to five transfers, for the most part by bus or by car, and also to two stages in a single day. But this time the riders rebelled. They'd had a hard day to St Lary-Soulan in the Pyrenees, where Mariano Martinez had won at five in the afternoon. Their hotels were down in the valley, in Tarbes. Thousands of spectators were going the same way, so Goddet and Lévitan had arranged for riders to use the cable car installed for skiers. That would take them into St-Lary itself but there they would still have to climb into buses to reach Tarbes.

The problem was that the riders were now down at the bottom but their buses were still at the top, or at best creeping down through the human tide. The riders therefore didn't get to their hotels until 9 p.m., others supposedly not until 11 p.m. To reach them had taken six hours, or as long as Martinez had taken to ride the stage. To make it worse, the delay hadn't been foreseen; the buses had little food or drink. They weren't the specialist, luxury buses that teams enjoy now. Their seats were fine for tourists but cramped after six hours' racing and then hours of hanging about waiting.

Some riders didn't get to bed before 1 a.m. once they'd been massaged and fed. And yet the Tour demanded they were out of bed at 4:30 next morning to have breakfast before starting a half-day stage to Valence d'Agen at 8:00 and then continuing to Toulouse in the afternoon. In all they were to ride 254 kilometres. The riders quickly agreed that this wasn't what they wanted.

Dirty Feet

Valence d'Agen, a community of 5,000 along one side of the Garonne valley and not to be confused with the larger Valence in the south-east of the country, had paid a lot of money for so tiny a place. The mayor, the council and everyone else lined the road for the great day. Instead, the bunch crawled towards them at little more than 15 kilometres per hour. "It just wasn't on," Bernard Hinault said with uncharacteristic understatement. It was his first Tour but he was already national champion and he had power. "Everyone was tired and so it was easy to get the whole peloton on strike," he said in *Le Peloton des Souvenirs*. "We rode at walking speed. Some of the riders were riding through the fields and others were stopping to buy drinks."

The heroes were fighting back. Goddet begged them to race first and argue afterwards. But the riders had already protested the previous day and been dismissed and some had asked for the stage to be delayed, shortened or even cancelled. With the riders sticking to their protest, Goddet then threatened to withhold the morning's prizes, which did nothing to lighten the mood. He then told André Chalmel, a teammate of Hinault's and the president of the riders' union, that he'd hand over the money if they'd race the last 30 kilometres. But it was too late. "We're not circus animals," he protested.[190]

The riders crossed the Garonne from the south, ambled up the short rise to the town and turned into the boulevard Victor Guilhem. And there they stopped a hundred metres from the line, dismounted and walked the rest of the way, close to where the entrance to the Casino supermarket is now. In the front line were Michel Pollentier in his polka-dot jersey, Hinault on his left and beyond him Freddy Maertens in the sprinters' green. The people were angry. Some threw tomatoes. The mayor, Jean-Michel Baylet, a big cheese who went on to become a secretary of state and who happened to run the region's daily paper that had built up the big day, picked on Hinault and yelled abuse, screaming that he was besmirching the jersey of national champion.

More tomatoes flew and Hinault climbed in among the protesters to sort them out. And still Goddet was intransigent: he cancelled the stage and told reporters: "It's necessary to keep the inhuman side to the Tour; excess is necessary." He also said that the early start had been for the riders' benefit, to let them race in the cool of the morning and give them plenty of time to eat and relax at mid-day. Few believed him; Valence is further from Tarbes than Toulouse and the two stages together made for a long day, of which the second half would be in the sun anyway.

The riders won. There were no split stages the following year and before long they'd gone. The press for the most part sided with the riders. *Le Monde* reminded readers of the Pélissier affair and the bar at Coutances, saying that that had "alerted opinion half a century ago to the extravagances of despotic regulations." *Le Matin* in Paris decried the Tour as excessive and dangerous. *L'Humanité* predictably described riders as the *smicards du vélo*, a *smicard* being someone employed for the minimum wage. Writers generally sided with Chalmel's claim that professional cyclists were workmen like any other, that they too were subject to and beneficiaries of labour laws, and that they had the right to strike. In the afternoon, Hinault was still wounded by the mayor's insults and he set off on a wild attack to show that he and nobody else would decide who and what brought honour to the blue, white and red of the national jersey.

Public reaction was less favourable. Most fans believed that riders were well paid and well rewarded. They lived a pampered life of hotels and free food and massage and they were doing a job they loved. They didn't see professional cyclists as similar to themselves and their everyday jobs in offices and factories. It all blew over in the end, of course. Hinault apologised to Baylet for spoiling his town's big day, the Tour offered Valence the morning's prizes to help its work with the old, sick and poor, and the riders came back to ride a race for nothing.[191]

It was the beginning of the end for an era of the Tour and its shameless search for money and any novelty that would bring in a cheque. Lévitan had begun taking anything that anyone would offer, putting him in line with many an organiser of humble amateur events. His lack of shame came to a ridiculous height in 1976 when the Tour began giving not money prizes but seaside apartments put up by Guy Merlin, a property magnate. His name was everywhere in the Tour. Over the years, Lucien van Impe, Bernard Thévenet, Joop Zoetemelk, Laurent Fignon, Greg Lemond, Stephen Roche and Pedro Delgado could all have had their summer breaks at Merlin's expense.

To promote his investments, Merlin had persuaded the Tour to visit St-Jean-de-Monts and St-Hilaire-de-Riez in 1972, 1975 and 1976. The last was given in Tour documents as Merlin-Plage but search for it on a map of the Vendée and you'll search in vain. It was a Merlin invention, a vacation centre at which he sold apartments. Such was the way in which Merlin dominated that the mayor of St-Hilaire was furious that his town didn't get a mention in Tour publicity and he called Lévitan to say so. Lévitan in turn pointed out that stage towns had to pay to have the race visit: if the mayor wanted to pay the bill instead of Merlin, he'd change the publicity, but until then the mayor would be better to keep his peace.

Merlin said his apartments were worth 100,000 francs but that, of course, was his valuation. If you didn't want an apartment and would have preferred the cash, the value was a lot lower. In 1988, Delgado won not just his apartment but a Peugeot 405 and an *objet d'art* as well as such cash as the Tour budget could spare.[192]

Unable to expand further in France, Lévitan yearned for *mondialisation*, a Tour starting in America, crossing Britain and circling the continent before spending the last five days in France. Every fourth year, he said, the USA, Canada, Portugal, Poland, Colombia, the Soviet Union, Czechoslovakia and a handful of African countries would be allowed to field amateurs. None of it happened. There weren't enough Concordes to get riders from America to Europe without crippling jet lag, the eastern Europeans had no intention of being polluted by capitalist professionalism, and there just weren't enough riders in Africa. In the end, only the Colombians turned up.

When Jonathan Boyer rode the Tour as its first American, in 1981, Lévitan insisted he wear not his Renault team jersey but a Stars and Stripes to which he wasn't entitled, because he hoped it would bring interest and money from across the Atlantic. It was this obsession with America that cost him his job in dramatic style.

Lévitan had come into his own when Émilien Amaury bought *L'Équipe* and the Tour in May 1965. Amaury, who you'll remember had run *Parisien Libéré* as a workers' cooperative, had since moved far to the right. He became so unpopular among his employees and journalists in general that a strike kept *Parisien Libéré* off the street for three months in 1970. Relations became ever more bitter, to the extent that when he died in a riding accident in a forest at Chantilly in 1977, the left-wing *Libération* had the huge headline: "Amaury's horse unhurt in accident" followed by the much smaller line: "The rider, owner of *Parisien Libéré*, did not survive his injuries."[193] The caption beneath a front-page picture of a horse, presumably the one in question, pointedly said: "As bad a horseman as he was a driver, Mr Amaury had recently taken up horse-riding after the suspension of his driving licence." The satirical magazine *Charlie Hebdo* went further. Over a cartoon of Amaury's face in his coffin, beneath a horseshoe, its front-page headline was simply: "A bastard is dead."[194]

The turmoil didn't end there. French law insists that a parent's belongings on death are shared equally between his children. Amaury wrote a will that favoured his daughter, Francine. Six years of legal battles ended with the son, Philippe, inheriting the papers and Francine the magazines. Émilien Amaury was neither loved nor missed, including by his children.

Philippe, now owner of the papers, looked on Lévitan less indulgently. He gave him the push on the morning of 17 March 1987. Lévitan came in to work to find the lock to his office changed and a court bailiff waiting to clear his desk amid claims, never proved, of financial mismanagement. The claims against him were as complex as financial arrangements always are but the essence is that he was said to have used the Tour's money, perhaps as an investment, perhaps as a loan, to start a Tour of America. Claim and counter-claim followed. The outcome was that Lévitan couldn't get into his office and he walked back out into the street no longer an organiser of the Tour de France. There then began a long sulk which ended only when he paid a surprise visit to the Tour in 1998. He died in 2007, aged ninety-five.

Lévitan was a man of charm but someone with whom few people felt at ease, according to the Tour's doctor, Gérard Porte. A room could fall silent when he entered.[195] He admired everything British even though he never mastered the language or showed any inclination to go to Britain more than he had to. When he took the Tour there, it was only because the fledgling Brittany Ferries and a group of farmers seeking to sell artichokes paid him to. He drove a Jaguar on which he stuck paper labels in French to explain the choke, heater, starter button and the other controls.

Goddet left a year after Lévitan. A towering, gentlemanly presence to the end, he also died at the age of ninety-five. He is buried in the cemetery at Passy, in Paris's twelfth borough. He had been at first *L'Auto* and then *L'Equipe* since 1924. He followed every Tour until 1989, with the exceptions of 1932 when he went to the Olympic Games in Los Angeles, and of 1981, when he was ill.

> VOICES FROM THE PAST
>
> He was one of the inventors of French sport.
>
> —President Jacques Chirac

> VOICES FROM THE PAST
>
> [Jacques Goddet] made the Tour de France, through his fifty years at its helm, the most popular French sports event and the one most known across the world.
>
> —Prime minister Lionel Jospin

11
Fresh broom

A sense of shock fell over the Tour, both organisers and riders. Nobody knew what should happen next. It had been so long. The succession had always seemed so obvious, the continuity of tradition so established. The race passed from organiser to organiser and for a moment called itself just Le Tour. It took another journalist, Jean-Marie Leblanc, to create what it is today. He did away with the tinpot sponsors and the endless finish line presentations that justified their investment but continued after most of the crowd had gone home. Above all, he gave the Tour a sense of dignity, of self-respect.

"My first preoccupation has been to restore the Tour's sporting credibility," he said. "We have simplified the Tour, which had become incomprehensible to the public. Cutting the number of *partenaires* has increased their visibility, which means we can charge them higher prices and so offer better prizes. We want to match the sort of prizes offered in the greatest sports events in the world."

To do that, he cut the number of trophies from twelve to six: that for the overall leader, which remained the most important, the competition for winners of stages, then the polka-dot jersey for best climber and green for best sprinter, and a white jersey for the best young rider, plus best team: all competitions which maintained interest throughout the month.

His other distinction was that he had himself ridden the Tour and then been the voice of Radio Tour, the race's internal news service. And a single story shows what a difference that makes. "I remember the year that the Colombians were riding," he said. "I passed in front of the hotel where they were staying. I saw them queuing up outside a phone box. I saw them using coins to phone home. I was angry: cyclists riding the Tour have to rest. From then on, we arranged that there were phones in all the riders' rooms." He also knew another side of riders' life: in 1970 he and other riders were fined when they stopped for a picnic under a tree, a publicity stunt for their Bic team.

Cyclists once had been largely half-literate, grunting men who preferred the hard labour of the bike to the other life that awaited them, in a factory or in a field. There *were* literate, articulate racers, of course, but the justified stereotype of an everyday bike rider until a decade after the peace of 1945 was that of a punch-drunk boxer. By contrast, Leblanc studied law and economics at Lille University. A reporter from *Sud-Ouest* pointed out that Leblanc was the first bike-rider he'd met who could talk in the subjunctive imperfect, a tense that defies not only non-native speakers but most native ones as well.

He rode his first race, with unlicensed amateurs, in 1961. The following year he won his first proper race, at Bousies, between Lille and Reims. He was still at the Lycée Dupleix at Landrecies, taking the philosophy section of his *bac*, the biggest examination at a French school and the one on which all other examinations depend. "I knew nothing about cycling," he remembers. "Nobody even told me not to wear underwear under my shorts, so that I rode my first race with underpants, with chamois and in cycling shorts. In fact, all I knew about cycling was what I'd learned from Jean Bobet's book, *Champion Cycliste*."

In 1967 he had a semi-professional contract for the following year. But there'd be no money until the season began. He was delivering boxes for a chocolate factory to pass the time and earn some money and he nervously asked the sports editor of *La Voix du Nord* if he could work there part-time. Seeing his name in print for the first time was "just like winning a race."

He remembers the start of the Tour de l'Hérault in south-east France and noticing nervously that Tom Simpson was sitting next to him. "Can you imagine that? You're a little amateur semi-professional and the professional champion of the world, with the rainbow jersey on his back, chats to you as though you're mates!"

The last man to win the Tour in a national jersey was the Dutchman, Jan Janssen, in 1968. National teams had returned for two years, again as a way to punish sponsors, who in this case were held responsible for the riders' strike at Bordeaux, protesting drug controls. Only four of Holland's ten starters made it to Paris and the council track in

Vincennes: the rest abandoned their leader and went home to fill their time and their pockets by winning money in round-the-houses races in Belgium.

Leblanc rode that Tour as his first, not in the French first team but for the Bleuets, the second-strings led by Lucien Aimar. Outside the Tour, he rode for the Pelforth brewery, alongside Janssen. But France was rightly concerned by its alcohol problem and it banned breweries from advertising in general and from sponsoring sports teams in particular. He and Janssen went to Bic, sponsored by a maker of ballpoint pens and razors, under the management of Raphaël Géminiani. The 1970 Tour was Leblanc's second and last—he finished eighty-third. "If you want me to say that I dreamed of winning," he said in an interview with *Vélo*, the monthly he once edited, "the answer is no. I just didn't have the class. There were riders like Tom Simpson, like Eddy Merckx, like Luis Ocaña in the same peloton as me, so I can't do otherwise than say that, by comparison, class was what I lacked."

A week after he retired as a cyclist, he went back to working at *La Voix du Nord* and he followed his first Tour as a journalist in 1974. That brought him a job at *L'Equipe* and then the editorship of *Vélo,* its monthly magazine. He was there when Jean-Pierre Courcol, a former PR man who'd become the Tour's organiser after the Lévitan business and Goddet's retirement, suggested towards the end of 1988 that Leblanc become the race director, the man running the Tour on the road. And it was from there that he became the overall organiser when Courcol left in 1993.

Leblanc was the first organiser to retire as soon as he'd paid enough in taxes for his pension. He may be glad that he did retire; though no reflection on him, his time was marked by crises. His first, which briefly reduced him to tears of frustration, was what became known as the Festina scandal. It started when a personable Belgian soigneur called Willy Voet, pronounced *Foot*, was stopped at an obscure crossing from Belgium into France with a stash of drugs intended for Festina, his team. It says something of the times that Voet took cocaine, heroin and amphetamine just to drive the short distance from Belgium to the port at Calais, and that he had a further supply tucked into his underpants. It was that that worried him when he was stopped, that the police or customs staff would spot that he was as high as a kite. He had injected himself from a phial without even knowing what was in it. “I knew it had amphetamine and that was good enough for me,” he said.[196] That in itself showed how ready drugs were and how flippantly they were regarded.

How he was stopped in an era of open borders remains a mystery. And we enter now a world of intrigue and backstabbing. The Tour that year started in Dublin and there was a reception in the gardens of Phoenix Park, the residence of the Irish president. It was Friday 10 July. Word of Voet’s arrest had reached Dublin and insiders were asking each other in whispers if they knew anything more. Among those most interested was Bruno Roussel, the team’s balding manager, “not the first man to seek the headlines,” according to another rider, Erwann Menthéour. There, too, was Marie-George Buffet, France’s elf-like sports minister. The two had met before and Buffet gave him a smile. A knowing one, as it turned out. Knowing because, unlike anyone else at the reception, she knew not only about the arrest but the analyses of what had been found in Voet’s car.

That evening Voet’s wife called to say that her husband was in jail and being questioned. Roussel engaged a lawyer in Paris. He had not yet thought of a link between Buffet’s smile and the calamity that was opening. Buffet was a communist in a broad-Left coalition under prime minister Lionel Jospin. She was appointed in June 1997, a year before the Festina scandal. Hers was only a minor appointment but she wanted to make a name for herself. She crusaded against drugs, having gone through all the earlier laws and history and decided they were insufficient in detail or practice. She wrote her own laws and proposed tighter controls for the Tour and elsewhere, attracting what she called pressure “of all sorts” when she insisted on a drugs check for the national soccer team in training for the World Cup in 1998.[197] Buffet, a member of the communist party since 1969 when she was twenty, was a left-wing politician in an intensely capitalist world.

Roussel’s lawyer explained what he saw as the link. Festina’s downfall, he said, began not when Voet drove through the Belgian border but months earlier in April. The prime minister, Jospin, was a socialist but the way votes had turned out in the election meant that he was obliged to work with a conservative president, Jacques Chirac.

Agnès Pierret, the administrative director of the Tour, had asked Festina if Chirac's wife could watch the team try the time-trial course in her home *département* of the Corrèze. Chirac had the support of Jean-Marie Leblanc, and the brassy Bernadette Chirac was calling on that friendship. She knew she would attract television coverage if she followed France's favourite rider, Richard Virenque, and that that would put her husband in a good light politically and bring publicity to a poor, sparsely populated area. Roussel resisted but buckled when Leblanc himself came on the line. And so on 23 June, Bernadette Chirac and Virenque were happy to pose for as long as the photographers asked.

The film never went out. The Chirac publicity machine was halted. Transmission was due for 18 July but that was the day, in the back room of the Chez Gillou café, at St-Priest-de-Gimel, close to Gare-de-Corrèze, that Leblanc threw out the whole Festina team. Gilberte Boulegue, a red-haired, bespectacled woman who had run the bar since 1976, remembered: "The whole circus of the Tour had turned up around 11 p.m. to paint the line on the road for the time-trial. They worked all through the night. They came into the bar for a sandwich and a drink. We had hundreds of customers. We worked forty-eight hours non-stop."

The stage set off from Meyrignac-l'Eglise. The Festina riders still wanted to take part. But they couldn't and instead they entered the bar and asked for a back room and sent everybody else out. After a while, with the atmosphere in the room growing fetid for lack of ventilation, Leblanc arrived. "They sent me away," said Boulegue. "There were cameras and microphones everywhere. They climbed on the tables, everywhere. We tried to push them back but it wasn't easy." Leblanc went into the back room and told Virenque and the others that they were out.

"It was so strange," Boulegue said, "to see the riders like that." Virenque, his hair recently dyed blond, was in tears, insisting that he and the others had left the race for the sake of the sport, neglecting to mention that it was the race that had left them. "They were like small children caught doing something naughty," Boulegue remembered. Nevertheless, she joined the Virenque fan club, believing he had been made a scapegoat, and asked him to sign a copy of his book for her. From then until they left the bar in 2008, she and her husband, Gilles, signed copies of *L'Equipe* for tourists "who came to see us as though we were a national monument." Even Virenque came back to see where it had all happened.[198]

Roussel's lawyer never suggested anybody's personal involvement. But nabbing a soigneur and his drugs was a chance for Buffet to push through the changes she wanted. And in doing so, the more she could change, the more shame she of the far left could bring on Chirac and the previous government of the right. Roussel had worked all this out by the time of the Festina trial at Lille in 2000. By then Virenque had stopped insisting he was innocent, going back on the story that he had told in his book, *Ma Vérité*, and muttering the words *"Oui, je me suis dopé."* Being questioned by a judge uncaring of reputations had been different from dealing with toadying cycling writers. The mystery, however, widens.

Roussel went for dinner with a policeman involved in the case. Was he right, he asked, that Voet had been *balancé* [thrown to the lions] by someone within cycling?

"You understand that I can't really tell you," the policeman said.

Roussel mentioned a name, which he hasn't revealed.

"Sorry, I can't confirm that," the policeman said. But without denying it. Roussel says that convinced him it was a set-up from inside the sport. But nowhere in his book does he go further.[199] His story ends there. The link with Buffet and the border agents is unexplored.

Cynics would smile at what they'd see as his self-justification and say "Well, he would say that, wouldn't he?" But Roussel said nothing of the affair until 2001, by which time he had left the sport and had little need to defend his reputation. Leblanc's troubles, however, weren't over. The police, as unconcerned as the judge by the self-importance of riders and team officials used to being cheered and adulated, turned over hotels and searched suitcases and buses. The riders protested at what they considered heavy-handed treatment and on 29 July they sat in the road and sulked. Five teams went home. A little later the TVM team followed them. The shame was so great, and the field now so reduced, that *Le Monde* called for the Tour to be abandoned.

Virenque was sent home from the trial excused but was later fined 4,000 Swiss francs by the sport itself. The court fined Roussel 50,000

French francs and gave him a year's suspended prison sentence. Voet was fined 30,000 francs and also given a year's suspended sentence. Laurent Brochard, one of the riders involved, said long afterwards: "I'm still ashamed of the whole business. It keeps coming back to me. I'm not at all proud of it. I burned my jerseys. A fire, outside. It was symbolic. The clothes that I had at the time, all of it, I burned everything I had."[200]

So drug-ridden was that Tour that doping had become a black rite of passage. It didn't seem so at the time but the urine that riders provided certain that it would reveal nothing turned out, when tests were improved years later, to come back and haunt them. There were 189 riders when the race started and no fewer than 56 turned out later to have taken EPO, a drug that has the same effect on blood as coupling another locomotive has on an express train.[201] Given that only some of the riders were tested each day, that is quite some proportion. Some riders who weren't found positive have since been denounced by other riders, including their former team-mates. Such is the black cloud that has persisted since 1998.

Jean St-Marc wrote in the serious periodical, *Obs*: "The most prominent [*médiatique*] case was Laurent Jalabert. A broadcast consultant for RTL and France Télévisions since 2003, the former climbing champion, and fourth in the Tour de France in 1995, stood out particularly because of his defence of Lance Armstrong [later stripped of all his Tour victories after his persistent denials of drug-taking were shown to be lies]. 'Armstrong, however you look at it, is an immense champion… He's someone with enormous talent and mental strength.' When *L'Equipe* revealed that retroactive tests showed Jalabert positive for EPO in 1998, he gave up his work as a consultant."[202] Only to start again later.

Voet is still *persona non grata* at the Tour. He has had a stroke and lives now in retirement in the French Alps, still hoping that one day he will be invited back to a race where, he believes, he did no more than others and a good deal less than some. Roussel left the sport to sell houses but returned to manage the Mexican national team for two years. He now helps junior riders at Pontivy, in Brittany. Virenque resumed riding, had a bad crash on a mountain bike, tried his hand at making jewellery, and has been a commentator on television, originally in a difficult partnership with Cyrille Guimard, whose job, it was said, was to translate into French whatever it was that Virenque had just said. Festina felt itself untouched by the scandal because it didn't reflect on its clocks and watches and it is still a sponsor in the sport, although not of a team.

And then Armstrong—the man who won every Tour from 1999 to 2005 in a career which thrilled Americans who warmed to his recovery from cancer but often seemed too good to be true to Europeans. Over and over he challenged accusers with a simple question: would he, having recovered from cancer, risk his health and even his life by taking drugs?

"People ask what I'm on," said one of his endorsement advertisements on television, to which he said he was on his bike for hours day after day.[203] Only hard work, determination and talent did the job, was the implication. The second youngest man to win the world road championship, and more Tour wins than any rider in history, he took on the mantle of superman that Desgrange had always wanted. Time and again he rode away from the field on the last climb, turning a smaller gear than was fashionable and taking yet another yellow jersey.

But the way he treated friends came back on him. Another American, Floyd Landis, having himself been caught in a drugs test, asked Armstrong to take him into his team at the end of his suspension. Armstrong refused, but not sweetly. Landis was hurt and told all he knew, not just to anyone who'd listen but to a legal inquiry that already had its sights on Armstrong. Other old colleagues also turned on Armstrong. When his room-mate, Tyler Hamilton (no angel in doping either), described all he had seen, Armstrong told him he would make his life hell. When his masseur, Emma O'Reilly, spoke of how she had added make-up to Armstrong's needle marks, Armstrong publicly called her a prostitute and an alcoholic. Nobody who displeased Armstrong, still less got on his way, was left uninsulted and unthreatened. Betsy Andreu, whose husband said he felt forced to take drugs under Armstrong's team leadership, swore under oath that in 1996 she had heard Armstrong telling hospital doctors of all the drugs he was taking. They made quite a list: she said he had taken cortisone, testosterone, EPO and human growth hormone. Messages left on her answering machine by people associated with Armstrong included ones that said: "I hope someone breaks a baseball hat over your head" and "I hope you suffer some adversity in your life" and "You're a bitch."[204]

Wanting to get the subject into the open and perhaps hoping it would go away, Armstrong appeared in 2013 on a television programme run by the American presenter, Oprah Winfrey. In what sounded like a pre-arranged routine, Winfrey asked time after time if Armstrong had taken drugs, each time in a different circumstance. And each time, without hesitation, Armstrong said he had.

The skids had been under him since *L'Equipe* ran a front-page story headed "The Armstrong lie."[205] The paper's investigator, Damien Ressiot, had been able to bring together two sets of numbers: those of riders found to have taken EPO, which wasn't illegal at the time but which Armstrong had denied, and the numbers on the anonymous test bottles. Armstrong predictably dismissed *L'Equipe* as a tabloid, which it wasn't in either size or tone but which he could feel confident that his American fans would not know.[206] The story caused a sensation; there was a stream of cyclists riding across the border from Italy, Belgium and elsewhere to buy a copy.

The outcome was that Armstrong was relieved of all his Tour wins and the records now show just a dash where there should be a name. His private sponsors abandoned him and some sued to get their money back. He has already paid out more than $20 million.[207] His charity for cancer survivors, Livestrong, disassociated itself from its founder. Superman had fallen.

Jean-Marie Leblanc achieved his ambition of qualifying for a pension the year after Armstrong's last win. He wrote in his contribution to *Le Tour, 100 images, 100 histoires*: "We have been abused. I will say it again and I will stand by it: Armstrong cheated the Tour de France, the public, the media, all those who believed in the worth of his performances and, worse still, he has betrayed his sport."[208] He was the Bernie Madoff of cycling, he said, a reference to an American fraudster jailed for an investment scheme that tricked 4,800 clients out of $64.8 billion.

Leblanc is now back in northern France, one of 650 people at Fontaine-au-Bois, south-east of Arras near the Belgian border, where he became deputy mayor. That follows another tradition because Jacques Goddet and Félix Lévitan were also mayors of their home community.

Leblanc still plays the clarinet. He's no bad player, either: in June 2008 he played Mozart's clarinet concerto with the Salle Philharmonique du Conservatoire de Liège, across the border in Belgium. His bike-riding days have long gone, though. He and his wife have become long-distance walkers, having completed the Camino de Santiago, known in France as the Chemin de Compostelle, an old pilgrimage route that runs through France to the north-western tip of Spain. They have also walked the 250 kilometres of the Stevenson trail through the Cévennes from Puy-en-Velay to Alès.[209]

The tradition of entrusting the Tour to a journalist has continued, the latest being Christian Prudhomme.

Even though so many riders have fallen from grace faster than they rose, there have indeed been supermen in the sport. Not unsullied, it has to be said, but two riders stand out. Which you pick as the better depends largely on which generation you come from but both created an impact and a legacy to which others have come not even close. They were Fausto Coppi, whose career straddled the Second World War, and Eddy Merckx, who was of the generation born soon after peace returned.

Raphaël Géminiani said of Coppi that, at his peak, nobody needed a stopwatch to measure his wins: a church-tower clock would be just as good. The impact that Coppi created can be told in a simple tale. It starts with a man called Len Levesley, a London bike-shop mechanic who moved in his retirement to the mountains of the English Lake District. Like Coppi, he was in an army, although a different one—the RAF, in fact—but unlike Coppi he contracted polio. His two years in the North African desert were marked by taking showers from buckets of dirty water. It was from that, he believes, that he caught polio.

"I was stretcher-bound and there wasn't a lot I could do for myself," he said, "so one day I asked if someone could cut my hair for me. They said they'd send for an Italian prisoner of war to do it, because in wartime you grabbed anybody you could when you wanted something done. And I waited and then a few minutes later the tent-flap parted." Len looked round, half bored and in pain, to see who it was. And there, tall, hawk-like and out of place, stood not just an Italian prisoner of war but the greatest bike-rider in history: Fausto Coppi.

"Oh, I should think it took me all of a full second to realise who it was," Len laughed. 'He looked fine, he looked slim, and having been in the desert, he looked tanned. I'd only seen him in cycling magazines but I knew instantly who he was. So he cut away at my hair and I tried to have a conversation with him, but he didn't speak English and I don't speak Italian. But we managed one or two words and I got over to him that I did some club racing. And I gave him a bar of chocolate that I had with me and he was grateful for that and that was the end of it. On returning to Civvy Street a year later, the local club boys nicknamed me Holy Head," he laughed.[210]

Len's career peaked with a club record from Harrow to Buckingham and back, "for which I've still got the cup on the other side of the room, because nobody's tried for it since." Len held a record that interested no one and he was just another bike-rider among so many. And yet by contrast there were more than 300 metres of wreaths—nearly a quarter of a mile—at Coppi's funeral. A former cripple who believed he had been cured by a small sum that Coppi had given him walked all the way there. Some say the crowd was 100,000 strong. Jean Bobet, brother of Louison, wrote: "Since noon on Saturday, this crowd has filed past the last remains of the greatest champion we have ever known… As I write these words, hundreds and hundreds of people continue to file past in the muddy road."

Cycling in Italy did its best to keep Coppi out of the war and in 1942 he won the national road race and the national pursuit and broke the world hour record. But being at home and riding his bike while elsewhere Italians had for two years been attacking Greece and fighting in North Africa wasn't a comfortable position. His time was up when the 38th Infantry got a new colonel. Soldier 7375 of the Ravenna division was to report for duty.

Coppi's blind soigneur, a short, stout and jowly man called Biagio Cavanna, was desolate. Cavanna, in the mystique of the sport, is always portrayed as a genius and magician who could guide a man's career merely by stroking his legs. Cavanna was born in 1893 and died in 1961. He felt the first symptoms of blindness while riding a six-day at Dortmund in 1936. Claims that surrounded him, and which persist, are too fantastic to be true. Each was better than the last, until it was said that he could simply sense if Coppi was leading a race. This was an era when fans and journalists wanted their heroes untainted, when people had far less understanding of medicine and physiology (doped riders often believed they had taken "vitamins") and when those working with riders were little better than witch doctors, charlatans and drug dealers of a scale that these days would put them in jail. In reality, Cavanna knew a bit about drug cabinets and he suggested that Coppi soak a cigar in some concoction of his own invention and hold it under his arm so the contents would soak into his skin.[211] That would make him sick enough to avoid being sent to Africa.

Coppi refused and in March 1943 he sailed for Tunisia. "No one had much confidence in the outcome of the war," he told a journalist afterwards. "Defeat was marching towards us in seven-league boots and everyone knew it." He went south to face the British at Mareth, south of Gabès in Tunisia. He and the others were cut off. Their commander began praying loudly to the Virgin Mary and soldiers began shooting into the air "for no reason other than to make a bit of noise." On April 13, Coppi's war career ended a month after it had started. The British took him prisoner. Many Italians were happy with that. Few of them wanted to escape and rejoin the fighting and Coppi talked cycling at night, and shared meals and a plate with Arduino Chiappucci, the father of Claudio, a star of the 1990s. By day he drove a truck that the British taught him to operate.

On 13 October 1943, Italy changed sides. Prisoners could now be allowed back to Italy once the Germans had been cleared out. And so in February, 1945, truck driver Coppi was posted to an air force camp near Naples. And there he became batman to a British officer who cared nothing about cycling and wasn't bothered by his charge's fame. Provided he could polish boots and keep the place tidy, he'd get all the recognition he deserved.

A local footballer did recognise Coppi, however, and he passed the news to *Il Mattino,* which added to the tale by reporting that Coppi was "training furiously." A man called Nulli,[212] who had a bike factory in Rome, went to the now friendly British and asked to visit their prisoner. In his pocket he had 12,000 lira which, slipped into Coppi's hand, became his contract to ride for a year in Nulli colours. "I can never express the gratitude I feel to that kind-hearted man who gave me back my happiness", Coppi recalled. And the British? Well, what did it matter if a prisoner went out on his bike? All they asked was that he didn't go further than Rome.

This wasn't the Coppi people remembered. He had had a first bout of the malaria that eventually killed him. "I'm only a shadow of how I used to be", he wrote to a friend. "I'm scared of the future. But one step at a time; all I want at the moment is to get home."

He rode his first race on the Appio track in Rome and got 16,000 lire. There were more races but rarely more in prizes than local fans could scoop from their pockets. And then the war ended for Italy. So he pedalled north. A bunch of soldiers pulled him aboard their truck, delighted at their celebrated companion. "The truck was chock-full of prisoners and internees," Coppi remembered. "I found a place at the rear of the platform with my legs hanging over the tailgate. Suddenly there was a violent pitch that threw me out of the truck and on to the road. When I came to, the truck had gone. All that was left of it was a tangle of scrap metal 200 metres below me at the bottom of a ravine, with dead bodies lying around."

Coppi won the Grand Prix des Nations, Milan–San Remo and the Tour of Lombardy in 1946, the Giro, Nations and Lombardy in 1947, Milan–San Remo and Lombardy in 1948, the Tour de France, Giro, Milan–San Remo and Lombardy in 1949. Eddy Merckx once said: "It is flattering for me to be called the best in the world, but what would Coppi have achieved if he had not lost six years to the war?" And, long after it had ended, it was that war that killed him. He had caught malaria and, like Len Levesley's polio, it never left him.

In December 1959, the west African state of Burkina Faso was celebrating a year of independence. Until then it had been Haute-Volta. The president, Maurice Yaméogo, invited Coppi, Géminiani, Anquetil, Bobet, Roger Hassenforder and Henry Anglade to race and hunt. At Fada N'Gourma, 230 kilometres west of the capital, the party turned in boozily for the night before a safari in the Porga game reserve. Géminiani remembered: "I slept in the same room as Coppi in a house infested by mosquitoes. I'd got used to them but Coppi hadn't. Well, when I say we slept, that's an overstatement. It was like the safari had been brought forward several hours, except that for the moment we were hunting mosquitoes. Coppi was swiping at them with a towel. Right then, of course, I had no clue of what the tragic consequences of that night would be. Ten times, twenty times, I told Fausto: 'Do what I'm doing and get your head under the sheets; they can't bite you there.'"

Both men caught malaria, although in Coppi's case it was re-caught. "My temperature got to 41.6," Géminiani remembers. That's 106 Fahrenheit. "I was delirious and I couldn't stop talking. I imagined or maybe saw people all round but I didn't recognise anyone. The doctor treated me for hepatitis, then for yellow fever, finally for typhoid." Nothing improved until a doctor who knew Africa took a guess and saved Géminiani's life. Doctors in Italy had no such insight and disagreed among themselves and Coppi died at 8:45 a.m. on 2 January 1960.

When Géminiani spoke of needing only a church clock to time Coppi's wins, it wasn't entirely exaggeration. Coppi won the 1952 Tour de France by 28 minutes 17 seconds, and that after winning the stages to Nancy, Alpe d'Huez, Sestriere, Pau and the Puy-de-Dôme. Jacques Goddet had to double second prize to keep any interest in the race.

Coppi, says John Foot, "was a spectacle, a show, a piece of theatre. He was always metaphorically on stage,[213] riding between packed rows of crazed fans up and down mountains, applauded and booed, loved and hated, touched and spat at, cried over, shouted at, patched up, whispered about. He was both pantomime hero and villain."[214] Geoffrey Nicholson wrote: "Round-shouldered and heron-like, he looked anything but an athlete, yet his physique perfectly suited his purpose: long slender legs, short body, the large thorax of an opera singer."[215]

The Sestriere climb portrays Coppi as Italians and, frankly, most other fans still see him. It is twelve kilometres long and, by the standard of these things, not especially hard. The stage straddled the border between France and Italy. Coppi could be a languid rider, and prone to crashes that broke bones. He rode hump-backed with a pained expression, his eyes hard and his nose like a falcon's beak. But on the Sestriere climb in 1949 he rode away from his rival, Gino Bartali, whose role as the traditional, religious son of the countryside was to be duplicated two decades later by Raymond Poulidor, and he won the day by close to twelve minutes. It brought him the Giro d'Italia and it explains Géminiani's reference to clock-towers.

Dirty Feet

> VOICES FROM THE PAST
>
> I took drugs only when necessary.
>
> And how often was that?
>
> Nearly all the time.
>
> —Fausto Coppi in a television interview

The mountain came into the Tour de France three years later, two days after the race's first finish on Alpe d'Huez, where Coppi had won alone. He rode off alone over the Croix-de-Fer, eased on the descent to let himself be caught by chasers, then rode on with them to the Télégraphe. And then on the Galibier he rode off alone ten kilometres from the top, leaving Géminiani, Bartali and Stan Ockers, a little Belgian, to whatever was left. He dominated so much that one day a minor rider called Jacques Vivier told reporters: "I thank Mr Coppi that he allowed me to win this stage in front of my people. Mr Coppi is a gentleman."

Coppi's race record speaks for itself but Italian radio commentators spoke even more. This was not a man but a god, an angel on wheels, perfect in every respect, crushing former wartime friend and ally alike for the glory of an Italy still blushing at Mussolini. Traffic jams began as listeners, some with radios in their cars—still a luxury then—tried to reach Sestriere. Police had to form a cordon along the finish straight to keep the road open. He won by more than seven minutes.

If you doubt the passion that Italians felt for cycling, for anything to lift them from the gloom, reflect on this: the country was in ruins, destroyed by both sides, and hungry men were fleeing to the cities or abroad. And yet, amid all this, Italy had no fewer than four daily newspapers dedicated solely to sport. A director of one of them, *La Gazzetta dello Sport,* wrote at his hero's death: "I pray that the good God will one day send us another Coppi."

But that was Coppi the Great. Not long afterwards, Coppi began an extra-marital love affair that had repercussions as high as the Pope in devotedly Catholic Italy. That, increasing age and doubtless the drugs took their toll. He was first to be dropped each day in the Tour of Spain. Promoters who engaged him often shortened their races just to make sure he was still there at the end. He had gone on too long. He was twenty when he first won the Giro, the Tour of Italy, and thirty-three when he last won the Tour de France. His obituary ran endlessly in *La Gazzetta* and for two pages in *L'Equipe*. The difference was that, in the French obituary, Jacques Goddet wrote: "We would like to have cried out to him 'Stop!' And as nobody dared to, destiny took care of it."

The magazine *Cycling* has its offices out in the suburbs of southern London these days but in the 1960s and 1970s it was above the Golden Egg restaurant in Fleet Street, then the heart of the British newspaper industry. It was just about the publisher's oldest magazine and the staff were convinced that the only reason it hadn't been closed was that the bosses didn't have the heart or, perhaps, that they'd never noticed the cramped, one-room office in which the staff worked was still there. In those days employees went out to races on Sunday and then returned to London to spend the evening editing other people's reports or writing their own. All unpaid, incidentally, because their wages covered only Monday to Friday.

One night they were confronted by a report from the world amateur road championship. It is a principle of journalism always to give a first name the first time someone is mentioned. Every other rider in a breakaway was named, or could be checked in reference books. But one rider defied the searches. All the staff knew was that he was Belgian—that and that nobody in Britain had heard of him and probably never would. So, joking that everybody in Belgium seemed to be called Willi, that's the name they gave him. And it's as Willi Merckx that the greatest rider of post-war cycling made his first appearance before the British.[216]

Few cyclists over the years have been handsome, but that's a frequent description for Eddy Merckx. He was taller than most—about 1 metre 62—with a mop of dark hair and slow-moving eyes beneath Betty Boop eyelashes. "Matinée idol" was a reference employed more than once. Often it was hard to make him out. He wasn't shy in crowds as Anquetil had been, and in private he was every bit as friendly. He wasn't arrogant—throughout his career his home phone number was in the Brussels directory—but he could seem aloof, and riders often mocked him behind his back for being a moaner, imitating his distinctive Brussels accent and occasional patois.

Yet team-mates often stayed with him even when they could have been in more elevated positions in other teams. Riding for and beside the dominant star had its appeal, of course: "He was such a consistent winner that it was like working for a man with a private mint."[217] And so frequent were those wins—one a week on average for six years—that he depressed the market in Belgium. Even if, as he mostly did, he rode for a foreign sponsor, potential backers at home saw less and less point in paying for a team if it was hardly ever going to win more than round-the-houses races. And since Merckx sucked up most of the good riders—Roger De Vlaeminck and Freddy Maertens were noticeable exceptions—there weren't too many stars left to make an impression.

He won the 1969 Tour by eighteen minutes. Belgium was in close to a national party. It had been a long time since Belgium won—three decades, to be precise, when Sylvère Maes led the field in by half an hour. In 1969 you could buy Eddy Merckx tea-towels even Eddy Merckx chewing gum. All this was helped in an artificially created country divided between Dutch-speakers in the north and French-speakers in the south by Merckx's coming from Brussels, in the centre of the country, as happy speaking Dutch as French.

In 1974, he won the Tour de France, the Tour of Switzerland and the Giro d'Italia in barely eight weeks. He won five of his seven Tours de France and spent ninety-six days in the yellow jersey. He led a charge on a stage into Marseille so fast that it finished before the mayor got there. Gaston Defferre took it as a snub and the race was banned from the city for the rest of his life.

That day, like all the others, there were no graceful tactics. He went to the front and defied the others to follow. He looked stylish in photos. To see him on the road, however, was different. His broad shoulders rolled like a boxer's, a style that fell short of ugliness but had none of the grace of Jacques Anquetil, Roger De Vlaeminck or Freddy Martens.

Like Coppi, though, Merckx also went on too long. And belatedly, he realised it. Driving home on 19 March 1978 from the Omloop van het Waasland, across the river Schelde from Antwerp, he turned to his soigneur, Piet De Wit, who was driving, and said that it had been his last race. He hadn't thought so when it began but his decision was taken by the time it ended. By then he had started around 1,800 races and won 525 of them.[218] Yet by the time he pulled on his jersey that day, he knew that his time had passed: C&A, a Dutch clothing store chain, had created a one-year team for him because nobody else wanted him, at least at the price he was asking. His last big sponsor, Fiat, would take him but only as the rider-manager of a youth team. Pride counts for a lot and it is not easy to be so dominant for a decade and then find yourself not exactly on the scrap-heap but not fought over either. "Willi" called it a day, went home, sulked, licked wounds, grew fat and then slim again, made guest appearances, started a bike factory and backed teams. He has since had a town square and a métro station named after him.

He was as close to Desgrange's superman that any man has been. He is not greeted now with the affection that meets Raymond Poulidor, but then he never was. Respect rather than warmth is what greets Merckx, and that is just as it should be.

In all this time, the Tour has covered more than 350,000 kilometres.[219] That's the distance from the Earth to the moon. It takes a hundred permanent staff, 300 part-timers, 300 team officials, 2,300 journalists, 600 caravan staff, 50 gendarmes of the *Garde Républicaine*, a dozen doctors, dozens of shifters of barriers, stages and loudspeakers to move it around the hexagon of the republic.[220]

It is a very different world from Desgrange's. Desgrange saw sport and the Tour in particular as social engineering. He wanted not just a cycling champion but a champion so mighty, so inspiring, that he would lead French youth out of their bow-legged, half-educated gloom. With that would come greatness for France.

Desgrange never spoke publicly in favour of what we now call social Darwinism, the belief that society should be manipulated so that the advancement of the strong over the weak could be accelerated. But that, through example if not force, was his aim. Desgrange wanted not so much a sport but, in his own words, a race so hard that only one man would survive. The survival of the fittest, therefore.

The notion that the Tour should be a spectacle, a challenge of speed, came late. To his dismay, no doubt, it came from a man he couldn't tolerate: Henri Pélissier. The most stubborn and perhaps most unpleasant rider that history has known pointed out what to us is now obvious:

that shortening each day's distance would provide the very thing that Desgrange wanted—that riders would make a race of it rather than saving their energy, clinging on as best they could, and then racing in just the final hour.

The Tour story starts with the Franco-Prussian war and the siege of Paris. Would he recognise his pioneering adventure in the modern race? Well, yes he would, because everything he contrived is still there. Other than the details, nobody has found a better way of doing it. His race has been copied round the world, not least because the Tour never thought to copyright the yellow jersey.

He would have been agog at the scale of the modern race, of course. He lived in an era before television so that the idea of Colombians and Turks and Australians watching his race would have perplexed him. Above all, he would be surprised and no doubt disappointed that independent judges and not the organisers governed the race.

He would wonder whether to take credit for the astonishing advances in health and life expectancy that accompanied his race. He would wonder how much he had helped that. He was born when half the children in France died before they were ten. Life expectancy was just twenty-five (though that is an average and the rate of childhood deaths influences it). At the start of the Tour de France, it had risen to thirty, although with the same caveat. By 2017, life expectancy was eighty for a man and eighty-five for a woman.[221]

Nobody seriously proposes that Desgrange or his Tour de France brought that about. But three things are clear: Desgrange set out on a noble mission that he never abandoned, that he just about found his supermen… and that he created a heck of a race.

Endnotes

1 Goddet, Jacques (1991), *L'Equipée Belle*, Paris, Robert Laffont-Stock, pp. 32–33
2 In Hubscher, Ronald (1994), *Les temps historiques du vélo*, L'Histoire, 178, p. 16
3 Héran, Frédéric (2014), *Le retour de la bicyclette*, Paris, La Découverte, p. 25
4 Some mystery surrounds the surname. Pierre's father is shown in genealogical records as Louis Michaut. Pierre, however, is always shown as Michaux. Both are pronounced the same way. It may simply be that it was the end of an era in which people wrote their names as they fancied.
5 Roberts, Derek (undated), *Pierre Michaux and his sons; the pioneers of the bicycle*, Kenilworth, England, Jim Willis, p. 3
6 Wilson, Harry, *The Times* (Scottish edition), 24 July 2017, p. 37
7 Cycling Theory and Practice (1891) in Roberts, Derek (undated), *Pierre Michaux and his sons; the pioneers of the bicycle*, Kenilworth, England, Jim Willis p. 5
8 Gilbert, Bentley (1965), "Health and politics: the British physical deterioration report of 1904", *Bulletin of the History of Medicine*, vol 39, no. 2, March-April 1965, pp. 143–153
9 McShee, George (1903), *The 19th Century*, May, p. 798.
10 BBC, "Bitesize", www.bbc.co.uk/bitesize/intermediate2/history/cradle_to_the_grave/liberal_reforms/revision/3/
11 *Life expectancy in France*, Institut National d'études démographiques, France, 2017
12 Cefalo, Eric (2002), *19th century working class conditions in France: clothing and its significance*, Department of history, University of Kentucky
13 Ross, Jonathan (2002), *Housing conditions of French workers*, Department of history, University of Kentucky
14 Ross, Jonathan (2002), *Housing conditions of French workers*, Department of history, University of Kentucky
15 Polansky, Iva (2017), "Victorian Paris", https://victorianparis.wordpress.com/tag/living-conditions-in-19th-century-paris/
16 Desgrange, Henri, *L'Auto*, 20 July 1903
17 Wheatcroft, Geoffrey (2003), *Le Tour: a history of the Tour de France*, London, Simon and Schuster
18 It's at 12 avenue Trudaine in the 9th arrondissement, or borough. It's now called the Collège-lycée Jacques-Decour, renamed after a teacher who fought in the Resistance.
19 Outside English-speaking countries, gear sizes are the distance covered by each turn of the cranks. A gear of 4.70m closely equates to 48 teeth on the chainring and 22 on the sprocket, which would be 58 inches by the imperial system. The comparison is close enough as an example but not exact. By contrast, Bradley

Wiggins used 58 x 14 for his attempt on the hour record in 2015, which is around 8.75 meters.

20 Cycling slang for exhaustion brought on by too little too eat: what marathon runners call "the wall"

21 Fife, Graeme (1999), *Tour de France, the history, the legend, the riders*, Edinburgh, Mainstream, pp. 20–21

22 Lablaine, Jacques (2010), *L'Auto-Vélo, le journal précurseur du Tour de France*, Paris, L'Harmatann, p. 19

23 Nicholson, Geoffrey (2016), *The Great Bike Race*, Oxford, Velodrome p. 62

24 "C'est pour éviter qu'un quidam quelconque n'écrive un engagement au-dessus de ma signature"—in Goddet, Jacques (1991), *L'Equipée Belle*, Paris, Robert Laffont-Stock, p. 30

25 "Henri Desgrange crée *L'Auto-Vélo*", *L'Équipe*, 16 October 1900, http://blog.lequipe.fr/histoire/1900-henri-desgrange-cree-l-auto-velo/

26 Reid, Carlton (2014), *Roads were not built for cars*, England, Front Page Creations, p. 286

27 Reid, Carlton (2014), *Roads were not built for cars*, England, Front Page Creations, p. 285

28 Duncan published a book called *The World on Wheels*, in 1926. To call it comprehensive is an understatement: it weighed three kilograms.

29 The American cycling historian, Bill McGann, makes this interesting observation: "There is a lesson for us today. The Dreyfus affair was a terrible case of ethnic profiling in which an innocent man, fitting an ignorant set of prejudices, was wrongly convicted of a crime… Today, as we [in America] let a fearful and aggressive government set aside our precious and cherished constitutional rights, let us remember Alfred Dreyfus and that nothing is more important than justice. If we don't, our children will view us with the same contempt as we view Dreyfus' jailers." —McGann, Bill (2006), *The story of the Tour de France, Volume 1*, USA, Dogear Publishing, p. 5

30 Kuhlmann, Marie (2016), *Les chimères de l'exil*, Paris, Presses da la Cité, unnumbered

31 Cossins, Peter (2017), *Butcher, blacksmith, acrobat, sweep*, London, Penguin, p. 7

32 *Le Figaro*, Paris, 5 June 1899

33 Kessous, Mustapha and Lacombe, Clément (2013), *Les 100 histoires du Tour de France*, Paris, Presses Universitaires de France

34 Boeuf, Jean-Luc and Léonard, Yves (2003), *La République du Tour de France*, Paris, Seuil, p. 29

35 Motoring was so new that there was no established term. "Moting" was one choice at the time.

36 *L'Auto* also copied other aspects of its rival. It had the same number of pages—four—and the same size of page—55 x 66—and the same six columns.

37 Lablaine, Jacques (2010), *L'Auto-Vélo, le journal précurseur du Tour de France*, Paris, L'Harmatann, p. 17

38 Goddet, Jacques (1991), *L'Equipée Belle*, Paris, Robert Laffont-Stock

39 Seray, Jacques (1994), *1904: The Tour which was to be the last*, USA, Buonpane, pp. 5–6

40 Seray, Jacques (1994), *1904: The Tour which was to be the last*, USA, Buonpane, p. 7

Dirty Feet

41 Seray, Jacques (1994), *1904: The Tour which was to be the last*, USA, Buonpane, p. 7
42 McGann, Bill (2019), *The story of the Tour de France, Volume 2*, USA, McGann Publishing, p. 13
43 Cormary, Frédéric, "Tour de France: l'inventeur du Tour de France est... Lot-et-Garonnais", *Sud Ouest*, France, 23 July 2014
44 There were 130,000 registered bicycles in France in 1893, 300,000 in 1895, 375,000 in 1898, 980,000 in 1900, 2,240,000 in 1907, 300,000 in 1911 and 3,500,000 at the start of the First World War. A jump before 1907 is unexplained but could have been a change in accounting or a clampdown on untaxed machines. In any case, it is reasonable to assume there were many untaxed bicycles. One estimate says three per cent, plus bicycles belonging to the police, army and other public bodies. The figure for French sales in 2014 was 2,977,600.
45 Goddet, Jacques (1991), *L'Equipée Belle*, Paris, Robert Laffont-Stock, p. 21
46 Vigarello, Georges, "Le Tour résiste tout", *L'Équipe*, 11 July 2017
47 Boeuf, Jean-Luc and Léonard, Yves (2003), *La République du Tour de France*, Paris, Seuil, p. 74
48 Boeuf, Jean-Luc and Léonard, Yves (2003), *La République du Tour de France*, Paris, Seuil, p. 76
49 McGurn, Jim (1987), *On Your Bicycle*, London, John Murray, p. 158
50 Nicholson, Geoffrey (2016), *The Great Bike Race*, Oxford, Velodrome, p. 67
51 Reed, Eric, "Le Tour de France is losing traction in its homeland", *The Conversation*, 16 July 2014, http://theconversation.com/le-tour-de-france-is-losing-traction-in-its-homeland-29156
52 *Le Parisien*, 20 June 2012
53 Joly, Olivier, "Je vois des crépuscules qui tombent", *Le Journal du Dimanche*, 27 July 2003
54 In Woodland, Léo, *The unknown Tour de France*, San Francisco, Van der Plas, 2000, p. 115
55 Poisson, Philippe, "Un petit ramoneur devient un 'as de la pedale!'", http://philippepoisson-hotmail.com.over-blog.com/article-33032055.html
56 In *Le blog d'un grincheux grave*, "Tour de France, Je me souviens de Maurice Garin", http://grincheux.typepad.com/weblog/2006/07/tour-de-france-maurice-garin.html
57 Chany, Pierre (1997), *La Fabuleuse Histoire du Tour de France*, Paris, La Martinière, p. 46
58 Nicholson, Geoffrey (2016), *The great bike race*, Oxford, Velodrome Publishing
59 The best known advertiser in Britain was the American, Charles Atlas—real name Angelo Siciliano—whose ads featured his own impressive body in leopard-skin trunks accompanied by the appeal "Give me fifteen minutes a day and I'll give you a new body". The seven-stone weakling appeared in his British ads. Seven stones is ninety-eight pounds and a cartoon showed a small man unable to respond as a passing hunk kicked sand in his face in contempt.
60 Van Reeth, Daam, and Larson, Daniel (eds) (2015), *The history of professional road cycling*, Cham, Switzerland, Springer International
61 Chany, Pierre, and Cazeneuve, Thierry (1997), *La Fabuleuse Histoire du Tour de France*, Paris, Minerva, p. 863
62 Joly, Olivier, "Je vois des crépuscules qui tombent", *Le Journal du Dimanche*, 27 July 2003

63 Lewis, Robert (2017), *The stadium century: sport, spectatorship and mass society in modern France*, Manchester, Manchester University Press, p. 180
64 Sadler, Simon (1998), *The Situationist City*, Massachusetts, Cambridge, p. 25
65 The *Cipale*, as it was known because it was once the municipal track for Vincennes, was built in 1896 and later renamed after Jacques Anquetil, who rode his final race in France there. The Tour used it from 1968 to 1975. Paris, to which it had passed in the 1920s, neglected it and it fell on hard times. Campaigners calling themselves *Sauvons la Cipale* (Let's save the *Cipale*) campaigned for its renovation and finally had their way. The refurbished track opened in 2015 after three years' work.
66 Oram, Gerard (1883), *Worthless Men; race, eugenics and the death penalty in the British army during the First World War*, London, Francis Boutle
67 Wheatcroft, Geoffrey (2003), *Le Tour: a history of the Tour de France*, London, Simon and Schuster
68 *Brouette*—French for wheelbarrow
69 Brill, Marlene Targ, 2008, *Marshall "Major" Taylor*, Minneapolis, Twenty-First Century Books, p. 75
70 De Visé, Daniel, 2019, *The Comeback*, New York, Grove Press, unnumbered
71 He was born at Southwold, in eastern England, on 27 September 1869. His family was there on holiday. During a wide career, he represented the USA at the creation of the Union Cycliste Internationale in 1900. He was later the UCI's president. He was also founder of the International Boxing Union. He died at Montmorency, France, in February 1960.
72 A reference to an incident in Morocco, now largely forgotten, which was a prelude to the war
73 References to earlier battles now just names on memorials
74 Dupâquier Jacques (1988), *Histoire de la population française*, Paris, PUF
75 Interview with author, 1987
76 He moved to Paris in 1887, joined *Le Vélo* in 1894 and then worked for *L'Auto* from 1900 to 1918. He died in Paris in January, 1960. A plaque in his honour was placed at the summit of the Tourmalet in 2018.
77 In Diamant-Berger, Marcel, (1959) *Histoire du Tour de France*, Paris, Librairie Gedalge
78 Read, Eric (2015), *Selling the yellow jersey: the Tour de France in the global era*, University of Chicago Press, p. 38
79 Feuillet's first name was Emmanuelle. He turned professional to support his medical studies in Reims. Knowing his mother would be ashamed, he entered races as Ludovic. He died at Asnières in 1955.
80 Vigarello, Georges, "Le Tour résiste à tout", *L'Équipe*, 11 July 2017
81 Londres, Albert, *Le Petit Parisien*, 27 June 1924, pp. 1–2
82 Literally, "a matter of boots", but it doesn't translate. To be "upright in your boots" in French means to be unbudging in an argument, convinced of its rightness, standing up for yourself.
83 That went down as well with me as fresh butter on a tart.
84 Roman Catholics pray at representations of twelve stages or moments of the journey they believe Jesus experienced on his journey to crucifixion. "We have fifteen" is a reference to the days of racing.
85 That soon the sport will be made up of hopeless men and devoid of stars
86 *Bulletin de la statistique générale de la France*, July 1921, Paris, Ministère du

Travail, p. 342

87 de Mondenard, Jean-Pierre (2003), *Dopage: l'mposture des performances*, Paris, Chicron, p. 14

88 By 1992 the once clunky derailleurs had become electric. The first to use one was Philippe Louvet, using a prototype sold later as the Mavic Mektronic.

89 In 1903, riders were divided between *poinconnés* and *déhérités*. The first were not allowed to change bikes or any part of them and their machines were fitted with lead seals. The *déhérités*, individuals without factory support, were allowed to change bikes.

90 Christophe is credited with being the first to wear the yellow jersey, an afterthought during the 1919 Tour he didn't like because of the attention that it brought him. Philippe Thys, on the other hand, remembered being given a yellow jersey six years earlier, in 1913. More than that, he gave so much corroborating detail that the Tour's historians said they took his claims seriously but couldn't confirm them because all the pre-war paperwork had vanished as it was being moved south to escape the German invasion of 1940 and that nobody had thought to write about it in the papers. The Tour wrote that Thys was "a valorous rider...well known for his intelligence" and that his memories "seem free from all suspicion" but that, in the absence of a witness, "we can't solve this enigma".

91 *Sporting Cyclist* was a British monthly edited by J.B. Wadley that appeared from 1955 to October 1968, when it closed after 131 issues. For much of that time it provided the only lengthy insight that British cyclists had of racing on the European mainland.

92 https://www.youtube.com/watch?v=zJ8QCDyB3Mo

93 Lambot, Firmin, in *The Bicycle*, 24 March 1952, p. 6

94 Thompson, Christopher (2006), *Tour de France: a cultural history*, University of California Press, p. xvii

95 Mignot, Jean-François, "An economic history of the Tour de France 1903-2015", chapter 4 of Pomfret, Richard and Wilson, John (eds., 2016), *Sports through the lens of economic history*, Cheltenham UK, Edward Elgar Publishing; www.elgaronline.com/view/9781784719944.00010.xml. The film had its echoes in Les Triplettes de Belleville (2003), an animated cartoon in which a boy is given a bicycle to lift him from his depression and beats himself to near-insensibility to ride the Tour de France.

96 Chany, Pierre, and Cazeneuve, Thierry (1997), *La Fabuleuse Histoire du Tour de France*, Paris, Minerva, p. 163

97 https://birthmoviesdeath.com/2014/08/31/talkie-terror-the-transition-from-silents-to-sound

98 Radio Cité continued broadcasting until the day before the Germans entered Paris. By then it was broadcasting just news and air raid warnings. The Germans seized the studios and transmitters and used them for propaganda.

99 *L'Intransigeant* never found its feet after its initial success. It moved politically from left to right and then to the centre, losing readers all the time. After numerous changes, it became the celebrity magazine, *Paris-Match*.

100 Virot moved to Radio Luxembourg and died on a motorbike in the Tour of 1957 when his pilot, Roger Wagner, lost control on the stage to Ax-les-Thermes and plunged into a ravine.

101 Mignot, Jean-François (2014), *Histoire du Tour de France*, Paris, La Découverte, p. 75

102 Mignot , Jean-François (2014), *Histoire du Tour de France*, Paris, La Découverte, p. 102
103 Scales, Rebecca (2016), *Radio and the politics of sound in interwar France 1921-1939*, Cambridge, Cambridge University Press, p. 40
104 A folk song in Yorkshire dialect, improbably about a man on the windy moors without a hat, the consequence being his likely death, after which "then worms will come and eat you up". It is likely that Leducq didn't understand a word.
105 Breckon, M. (1993), *A wheel in two worlds*, England, privately published, p. 141
106 De Latour was born in New York in September, 1906, of a French father and Belgian mother. His parents moved to France when René was eleven and he appointed himself interpreter for American troops in Paris at the end of the First World War, saying that he sometimes escorted them to the Folies Bergère. He joined *Paris-Soir* in 1932 and profited from his bilingualism by freelancing in English, particularly for *Sporting Cyclist*. There is reason to think that he was born just plain Latour and gave himself the aristocratic "de" in America, where nobody would know better. And that the colour of his youthful adventures were much improved by the telling. He died in 1986 after a stroke.
107 Héran, Frédéric, "Le retour de la bicyclette", *La Découverte*, www.editionsladecouverte.fr/catalogue/index-Le_retour_de_la_bicyclette-9782707186812.html
108 The first appears to have been the football pools company, ITP, which supported a team in Britain after the war. British road-racing was outside the UCI's control at the time so there was no action. Small outside backers later appeared in legitimate racing in Spain but the sport was too small and too distant from the central administration to be troubled. The first major sponsor from outside the trade was the cosmetics maker, Nivea, and the biggest was St-Raphaël, a drinks company that eventually sponsored Jacques Anquetil.
109 Holland, Frances (2007), *Dancing uphill, the cycling adventures of Charles Holland*, UK, M-and-N Publishing. The other riders were the Londoner, Bill Burl, who soon dropped out, and a Canadian, Pierre Gachon, who abandoned on the first day. Holland rode unsupported for 2,000 miles before being halted by a flat tyre and a faulty pump.
110 The Tour eventually forgave him. Brocco retired to run a café and a bike club at Vire, in Normandy. The Tour passed through the town many times.
111 McGann, Bill and Carol (2019), *The Story of the Tour de France Volume 1*, USA, McGann Publishing, pp. 115–116
112 Desgrange, Henri, *L'Auto*, 16 July 1928
113 Maso, Benjamin (2003), *Het zweet der goden*, Amsterdam, Atlas, p. 76
114 UK national archives: www.nationalarchives.gov.uk/education/empire/intro/overview2.htm
115 Desgrange said he would have gone to as many as twelve in a team but he didn't have the money.
116 Desgrange, Henri, *L'Auto*, 1 July 1930
117 Maso, Benjamin (2003), *Het zweet der goden*, Antwerp, Atlas, 2003
118 Maso, Benjamin (2003), *Het zweet der goden*, Antwerp, Atlas, 2003
119 L'Humanité, France, 22 February 2013
120 De Latour, René, "The climber from Cannes", *Sporting Cyclist*, UK, March 1967
121 To be more accurate, Vietto gave Magne his wheel but it didn't fit. Their teammate, Georges Speicher, also stopped. Magne took Speicher's wheel and Speicher took Vietto's.

122 Laborde, Christian (2007), *Dictionnaire amoureux du Tour de France*, Paris, Plon

123 Piaf had a talent for passionate but unrewarding love affairs. She speaks in her autobiography of standing cold but in love to watch her champion cyclist lap the roads of the Bois de Boulogne in Paris. She does not name him. Assumptions that it was the track sprinter Louis Gérardin were confirmed when her love letters emerged in 2018. Piaf says of him that "Never has a man taken me as much and I believe I am making love for the first time." Gérardin, on the other hand, said that 48 hours with Piaf was more exhausting than a stage of the Tour de France.

124 Lablaine, Jacques, "Henri Desgrange, l'énigme de la sépulture", *La Dépêche*, 9 June 2013, https://www.ladepeche.fr/article/2013/06/09/1646052-henri-desgrange-l-enigme-de-la-sepulture.html; "Le créateure du Tour de France, repose-t-il bien à Grimaud?", *Nice-Matin*, 30 June 2013, http://archives.nicematin.com/derniere-minute/le-createur-du-tour-de-france-repose-t-il-bien-a-grimaud.1325340.html

125 Bartali, a believer, was in a sporting war with Fausto Coppi, an atheist. The pair divided the country. It was predictable which Pope Pius XII was going to favour. After staying notoriously aloof from the death of millions in German extermination camps, he refused to bless the Giro d'Italia while Coppi remained in it; Coppi was a married man known to be having an affair, a scandal that prompted the police to raid the house he shared with his lover to see if they were sleeping in a double bed.

126 France was split between the north and along the west coast, which were occupied by the Germans, and the south, which was nominally independent. Travel between the two was close to impossible.

127 Pétain was sentenced to death for collaboration after the war and after fleeing to Germany. His sentence was commuted to life imprisonment by the post-war president, Charles de Gaulle, who had served under Pétain in the army and who had himself been sentenced to death by Pétain.

128 Penot, Christophe (2002), *J'écris ton nom*, Paris, Cristel, 2002

129 The legal argument was that Pétain had dissolved the republic and founded another France. What happened during the war was therefore nothing to do with the France that existed before it and was re-founded after it. The embarrassing legal nicety was ended when Jacques Chirac, as president, acknowledged it as a stain on France, and that the round-up and incarceration of Jews had happened with French complicity and even enthusiasm.

130 Penot, Christophe (1996), Pierre Chany, *l'homme aux 50 Tours de France*, St-Jean-le-Blanc, Cristel

131 Pierre, Frédéric, *Le journal* L'Auto *under the occupation (1940-1944)*, university paper, Dijon, Université de Bourgogne

132 *L'Auto*, 4 November 1940

133 Pétain was sentenced to death for treason. His sentence was lightened to life in jail because of the intervention of de Gaulle, who feared the risk to public peace of demonstrations for and against. Times were already troubled enough.

134 Dalloni, Michel (2013), *Le Vélo*, Paris, La Boétie

135 Bobet, Jean (2007), *Le vélo à l'heure allemande*, Paris, La Table Ronde

136 Many riders also had reason to fear the Germans would uncover their smuggling and black market operations. Some, like Rik van Steenbergen, were open

about it when the fighting was safely over. The first Dutch *maillot jaune*, Wim van Est, was found guilty of smuggling a cow from Belgium. He told the court it had been night. He had found a rope and was astonished to find there was a cow at the other end of it.

137 Leulliot died in February 1982.

138 Leulliot's papers were found after his death to have included plans for a Tour of the World.

139 Startt, James, "On tour with the communists", *Bicycling*, 30 April 2010, https://www.bicycling.com/tour-de-france/a20023978/2009-tour-de-france-behind-the-scenes-3/

140 *Daily summary excerpt, reported communist drive to seize power in France and Italy*, Washington, USA, Central Intelligence Agency, 1 December 1947, https://www.cia.gov/library/center-for-the-study-of-intelligence/csi-publications/books-and-monographs/assessing-the-soviet-threat-the-early-cold-war-years/5563bod2.pdf

141 "Amaury, Emilien", *Universalis*, https://www.universalis.fr/encyclopedie/emilien-amaury/

142 Maso, Benjo (2003), *Wij waren allemaal goden*, Amsterdam, Atlas, p12

143 Maso, Benjo (2003), *Wij waren allemaal goden*, Amsterdam, Atlas, p11

144 Chany, Pierre (1997), *La fabuleuse histoire du Tour de France*, Paris, La Martinière, p346

145 Laborde, Christian (2015), *A chacun son Tour*, Paris, Robert Laffont

146 Le Touzet, Jean-Louis, "La colère noire du nain jaune", *Libération*, 5 July 2003, https://www.liberation.fr/evenement/2003/07/05/la-colere-noire-du-nain-jaune_438858

147 "How world war II shaped modern France", *Euronews*, 2015, http://www.euronews.com/2015/05/05/how-world-war-ii-shaped-modern-france

148 Rohrbasser, Jean-Marc and Rousso-Rossman, Martine, *1939–1945 une démographie dans la tourmente*, Paris, Ined, p. 278

149 The Americans also proposed aid to their Russian allies and their satellites. An engineered row ensured the Russians walked out, which American negotiators said was as well because they'd have had trouble persuading their government to provide the money if some were going to what by then were seen as countries that threatened them.

150 Anquetil, Jacques, *En brulant les étapes*, Paris, Calmann-Lévy, 1966, p. 28

151 Boucher died of a heart attack in 1993 when he was 83. His shop, on the roundabout at the Place des Martyrs de la Résistance, became a newspaper shop and then a public library. An apartment block built on the site makes it unrecognisable. The shop was where the Garden Color hairdresser's is now.

152 *Le Parisien*, 2 December 2014

153 In Woodland, Les (2000), *The unknown Tour de France*, San Francisco, Van der Plas, p. 100

154 Boeuf, Jean-Luc and Léonard, Yves, 2003, *La République du Tour de France*, Paris, Seuil

155 *Le Monde*, 16 April 2002, supplement p. 3

156 Fotheringham, William (2002), *Put me back on my bike*, London, Yellow Jersey, p. 128

157 The grandchildren of Louis Renault have fought in the courts to be compensated for the confiscation. Historians are divided, one camp saying that Renault did

not simply make tanks for the Germans, for which perhaps it had no choice, but made them with undignified enthusiasm. The other side says that Louis Renault (who had ninety-eight per cent of the shares) was not personally responsible for the decision and, in addition, that the company made trucks but only repaired tanks, which meant it had not supplied arms. The row goes on. If it interests you, there's a summary at http://www.lefigaro.fr/actualite-france/2012/11/21/01016-20121121ARTFIG00576-bataille-d-historiens-sur-la-collaboration-de-renault.php

158 Albert, Aurélie, "Le Clermontois Géminiani raconte dans un livre son amitié avec le cycliste Anquetil", *France 3*, Rhône-Alpes, 28 May 2017, https://france3-regions.francetvinfo.fr/auvergne-rhone-alpes/clermontois-geminiani-raconte-livre-son-amitie-cycliste-anquetil-1262295.html

159 Anquetil had a strange relationship with time. For him, a minute after 3 p.m. was not the same as 3 p.m.—not because he was pedantic but because he was a calculator. One of his talents was to drive through a series of linked traffic lights to arrive at each the moment it turned green. It was that ability that gives strength to his calculation for Alan Gayfer of how fast he would ride a British time-trial.

160 Rasmussen, N. (2006), *Journal of the History of Medicine and Allied Sciences*, pp. 288–323

161 Woodard, C. (1961), *Scientific training for cycling*, London, Temple Press

162 Jamieson, D. (2015), *The self-propelled voyager: how the cycle revolutionized travel*, USA, Lanham/Rowman and Littlefield, p. 17

163 Britain took the first three places, with Dave Marsh the winner, a feat not repeated until Graham Webb won a more conventional championship in 1968. The track championships were taken away and completed in France because of their unconventional organisation and the condition of the track at New Brighton, near Liverpool.

164 Chany, Pierre (1975), *La fabuleuse histoire de cyclisme*, Paris, Martinière, p. 451

165 De Mondenard, Jean-Pierre (2003), *Dopage: l'imposture des performances*, Paris, Chiron, p. 82

166 Fotheringham, William (2002), *Put me back on my bike*, London, Yellow Jersey, p. 144

167 Fotheringham, William (2002), *Put me back on my bike*, London, Yellow Jersey, p. 145

168 In Koomen, Theo, 1974, *25 jaar doping*, Leiden, Uitgeveriz Luitingh

169 There is a dispute over the extent, if any, to which drugs contributed to his death. While most reports say Jensen had taken amphetamine and that the autopsy showed that, some insist that the autopsy report—given only to his family–said he had died from heat exhaustion.

170 *Cycling*, UK, 28 October 1967, p. 13

171 *Daily Mail*, London, 31 July 1967

172 Manning died aged sixty in 1974.

173 De Mondenard, Jean-Pierre (2000), *Dopage: l'mposture des performances*, Paris, Chiron, p18

174 Peters, J. (2005), "The man behind the juice", *Slate*, https://slate.com/culture/2005/02/the-doctor-who-brought-steroids-to-america.html

175 *Cycling*, London, 12 August 1967, p. 19. Condor is a bike shop in central London. Carried away by one of its riders being included in the national team, its

website for a while boasted that a whole Condor team had ridden.
176 Fotheringham, William (2002), *Put me back on my bike*, London, Yellow Jersey, p. 151
177 "Zoom", *Organisation de Radioffusion Télévision Française*, 11 July 1967
178 Simpson, Tom (1966), *Cycling is my life*, London, Pelham
179 Report published by the public prosecutor, Avignon, 4 August 1967
180 Denson, Vin, in "Death of a British Tommy", *BBC Radio 4*, 1987
181 Fotheringham, William (2002), *Put me back on my bike*, London, Yellow Jersey, 2002, pp. 164–165
182 Ruys, Charles, "Desgranges yesterday—dope today", *Cycling* 26 August 1967, p. 20
183 De Mondenard, Jean-Pierre (2003), *Dopage: l'mposture des performances*, Paris, Chicron, p, 67
184 *Cycling*, UK, 2 September 1967, p. 6
185 Penot, Christophe, *La France Cycliste*, http://www.lncpro.fr/Default6_32.aspx?-HeaderID=4&ArticleID=grosskost-charly&DirID=grands-champions&Subtitle-ID=Equipes%20%3E&TriID=
186 Besson, Émile, *L'Humanité*, https://www.humanite.fr/node/161744. De Gaulle had been surprised to see that Anquetil's name was not on a list of those to whom he was to award the Légion d'honneur. When he asked why, according to Besson, an aide explained: "There are all those stories of doping." De Gaulle's response: "I don't know anything about that." The *Marseillaise* is the French national anthem.
187 Penot, Christophe (1996), Pierre Chany, *l'homme aux 50 Tours de France*, St-Jean-le-Blanc, Cristel, p. 97
188 De Mondenard, Jean-Pierre (2003), *Dopage: l'mposture des performances*, Paris, Chicron, p. 217
189 Quoted *Cycling*, 22July 1967, p. 4
190 *L'Equipe*, 13 July 1978
191 Thompson, C., *The Tour de France, a cultural history*, Los Angeles, University of California Press, p224
192 The first prize in 1935 was never publicised. It happens to have been the equivalent of 1,600 euros but nobody said so, to save the winner tax problems. It's shown in the records as *non communiqué officiellement.*
193 *Libération*, 3 January 1977
194 *Charlie Hebdo*, no 321, 1 January 1977
195 Porte, Gérard (2011), *Médecin du Tour*, Paris, Éditions Albin Michel,
196 Voet, Willy. (1999), *Massacre à la chaine*, Paris, Calmann-Lévy, p. 25
197 *L'Humanité*, 21 March 2013
198 "Tour de France: la patronne du bar Chez Gillou, à Gare-de-Corrèze, an assisté en 1998 à l'exclusion de l'équipe Festina", *La Montagne*, 6 July 2016, https://www.lamontagne.fr/tulle/sports/cyclisme/2016/07/06/tour-de-france-la-patronne-du-bar-chez-gillou-a-gare-de-correze-a-assiste-en-1998-a-lexclusion-de-lequipe-festina_11989960.html
199 Roussel, B., 2001, *Tour de vices*, Paris, Hachette Littératures
200 Fralon, J-A, (2018), *Les secrets du Tour de France*, Paris, Vuibert, unnumbered
201 "Que sont devenus les cyclistes dopés en 1998?", *L'Obs*, https://www.nouvelobs.com/sport/20130724.OBS0833/que-sont-devenus-les-cyclistes-dopes-en-1998.html

202 "Que sont devenus les cyclistes dopés en 1998?", *L'Obs*, https://www.nouvelobs.com/sport/20130724.OBS0833/que-sont-devenus-les-cyclistes-dopes-en-1998.html
203 https://www.youtube.com/watch?v=fxnqHvEbGnc
204 "Abusive voicemails left for Betsy Andreu by Lance Armstrong pal become evidence in federal probe", *New York Daily News*, 18 September 2010, https://www.nydailynews.com/sports/more-sports/abusive-voicemails-left-betsy-andreu-lance-armstrong-pal-evidence-federal-probe-article-1.441582
205 *L'Équipe*, 23 August 2005, p. 1
206 It has since become a tabloid, although not in style. *L'Equipe* is one of France's best-selling newspapers
207 "A timeline of Lance Armstrong's cycling career", *USA Today*, 19 April 2018, https://eu.usatoday.com/story/sports/cycling/2018/04/19/a-timeline-of-lance-armstrongs-cycling-career/33994779/
208 "Leblanc: Armstrong le Madoff du sport", *Europe 1*, 2 May 2013, https://www.europe1.fr/sport/Leblanc-Armstrong-le-Madoff-du-sport-708054
209 The route celebrates Robert Louis Stevenson's account of his journey through the Cévennes with a donkey
210 Interview with author, 16 March 2006
211 Ollivier, Jean-Paul, 1979, *Fausto Coppi, la véridique histoire*, France, Editions de l'Aurore
212 *Nulli* means zero in Italian and Coppi's new jersey had a large o on it.
213 In London he was literally on stage. The Best All-Rounder concert, to celebrate the champions of British time-trialling, once engaged Coppi to ride rollers on a revolving stage so that fans could admire and study his position and style.
214 Foot, J. (2011), *Pedalare! Pedalare!*, London, Bloomsbury, p. 100
215 Nicholson, Geoffrey (1991), *Le Tour*, London, Hodder and Stoughton, p. 129
216 *Cycling Weekly*, 7 December 1989
217 Nicholson, Geoffrey (1991), *Le Tour*, London, Hodder and Stoughton, p. 135
218 "Eddy Merckx and the last race of the Cannibal", *Velopress*, https://www.velopress.com/eddy-merckx-and-his-last-race/
219 Kessous, Mustapha and Lacombe, Clément (2013), *Les 100 histoires du Tour de France*, Paris, Presses Universitaires de France, p. 3
220 Kessous, Mustapha and Lacombe, Clément (2013), *Les 100 histoires du Tour de France*, Paris, Presses Universitaires de France, p. 6
221 "Life expectancy in France", *Institut National d'Études Démographiques*, https://www.ined.fr/en/everything_about_population/graphs-maps/interpreted-graphs/life-expectancy-france/

Index

www.ingramcontent.com/pod-product-compliance
Ingram Content Group UK Ltd.
Pitfield, Milton Keynes, MK11 3LW, UK
UKHW041830200726
13854UKWH00002BA/909

9 781736 749401